WOVEN TOGETHER

Weavers & Their Stories

GINGKO PRESS

WOVEN TOGETHER

Weavers & Their Stories

First Published in the USA and in Europe in 2020 by

GINGKO PRESS

Gingko Press, Inc.
2332 Fourth Street Suite E
Berkeley, CA 94710 USA
Tel: (510) 898 1195
Fax: (510) 898 1196
Email: books@gingkopress.com
www.gingkopress.com

Gingko Press Verlags GmbH
Schulterblatt 58
D-20357 Hamburg / Germany
Tel: +49 (0)40-291425
Fax: +49 (0)40-291055
Email: gingkopress@t-online.de

ISBN 978-3-943330-35-9

By arrangement with
Sandu Publishing Co., Ltd.

First published in 2020 by Sandu Publishing

Sponsored by Design 360° — Concept & Design Magazine
Edited and produced by Sandu Publishing Co., Ltd.
Book design, concepts & art direction by Sandu Publishing Co., Ltd.

Chief Editor: Wang Shaoqiang
Executive Editors: Maxine Chang, Ye Zijun
Copy Editor: Kim Curtis
Designer: Liu Xian
Sales Manager: Deng Baoyi

Cover Design by Wu Yanting
Front Cover Project by Hermine Van Dijck
Back Cover Projects by María Hernández, Evee Erb,
The Ninevites, Morgan Hale, Kate Park

info@sandupublishing.com
sales@sandupublishing.com
www.sandupublishing.com

Printed and bound in China

CONTENTS

PREFACE

This book, *Woven Together: Weavers & Their Stories*, presents the work of 24 artists and studios focused on woven designs. It gives you a glimpse into their craft and shows artists' workspaces. These weavers straddle the boundaries of craft, design, art and architecture.

The weavers profiled in this book are all very different from one and another. Every single person has their signature and uses the ancient technique of weaving in their own unique way. Their work varies from fine woven textiles to big woven artworks and fragile handmade baskets. It shows a broad view on the possibilities that weaving brings, but it also shows one common love, the love for the thread in all its aspects. That's the connection that we weavers share with each other.

Weaving is a complex subject and it's impossible to show every aspect of it in one book. But, fundamentally, weaving is the transformation of fabric through the interlacing between warp and weft, which cross each other at right angles. The warp threads are held parallel while the weft is passed over and under the warp to create a fabric. This technique is 1,000 years old. Even though the looms and the tools needed for weaving have changed during all those years, the basic idea of weaving never changed. Crossing threads will transform into fabric.

As shown in this book, weaving can take several forms. Often a weave is only seen as a flat piece of fabric, which is subsequently transformed into a usable piece. But contemporary weavers show just the opposite. The splendor often lies in the fabric itself and does not require any additions or finishing. The magic of crossing threads ensures that the beauty lies in the fabric itself. And that it stands on its own.

An important characteristic that every weaver needs is concentration. The process of preparing a warp and threading the loom can take several days. It is a process that requires a lot of patience and concentration from the weaver. But this slow hand weaving will transform into a deep connection between the maker and their loom. A tension arises between hands and the yarn, and between the parameters of the weaving techniques and the freedom to create something new, which means transforming ancient techniques into a modern and personal story.

Weaving is something that is best done alone. The process takes so much concentration and can so easily go wrong if you are distracted. Every little change in material and every little mistake in the threading or pattern can change the base idea of a weaver completely. Problem-solving is very often a big part of the weaving process. And that's why the process of weaving is all about the excitement around the unknown. It's what the Japanese people call "wabisabi," the way of life that celebrates the "perfect imperfection." Weaving is about recognizing the beauty in the imperfections and understanding that loveliness can be found in many surprising places. That's why hand weaving is so interesting for the makers themselves. It's about letting go of our base ideas and accepting the uncalculated imperfections. Embracing them is in the interest of the maker and the viewer. And beauty will be found in these imperfections.

On a personal level, my first weaving experience immediately made me dream about all the possibilities of the craft. But it took me several years before I truly understood the basics of weaving techniques. My weaving teacher, who is in her 60s, told me that one human life isn't enough to explore all the possibilities of weaving. And that learning about weaving is a never-ending story. The center of our interest in weaving is how to transform techniques that have existed for 1,000 years into a personal, modern story. It's about how to transform an ancient craft into art, design or architecture. Woven textiles have the power to be transformed into whatever the maker wishes them to be. This is why weaving is the technique of hope for me. The sensitivity of the thread and its infinite options for creation give a great sense of freedom.

As a designer of woven surfaces, I feel very touched by how wide the range of possibilities is in weaving itself. I would describe my weavings as poetic textiles. I combine the artisanal character of old weaving techniques with modern aesthetics. I don't invent new weaving techniques. I believe my work finds its character in my choice of colors and yarns. It's an inspiration to see how other weavers approach the technique and transform it into their personal story.

Woven Together: Weavers & Their Stories invites you into the creative world of weaving and offers you a rare view into the makers' works and studios. Every curious fiber lover, sensitive soul and interested mind will find in this book an inspiration for woven art and we welcome you to have a unique look into our work and lives.

Hermine Van Dijck
Woven surface designer
www.herminevandijck.com

“Weaving is about recognizing the beauty in the imperfections and understanding that loveliness can be found in many surprising places.”

Craft and Culture: A History of Weaving

Weaving has an extensive history as one of the oldest and most prevalent methods of textile production in the world. The process, appearance and utility of weaving have dramatically changed throughout human history, allowing many samples of woven textile to serve as anthropological tools. Still today, weaving is a unique cultural emblem, which embodies the materials, techniques and histories of regions across the globe. With evidence of weaving dating back to the Upper Paleolithic era, the history of woven textiles offers an extraordinary glimpse into past civilizations and cultures.

Weaving tools.
PHOTOGRAPHY: Evee Erb

Nearly every culture around the world has its own distinctive style of weaving that has evolved through necessity, material and aesthetic. From the resplendent motifs of Indonesian Ikat to American coverlets, a wide array of traditional weaving techniques have created a plethora of patterns across the globe. Spiritually charged by the time, labor and expertise with which they were created, many of these textiles are often adorned with colorful, ornate symbols that have been passed down from generation to generation as valuable talismans.

Accompanying these diverse textiles are numerous presentations of weaving in mythology and folklore. Archetypal goddess-weavers are seen throughout the world as an ancient theme entangling magic, fate and the divine with domestic, everyday life. Since long before the invention of the wheel, weaving has been forging connections between humankind and nature in both the physical and metaphysical realms.

With very few exceptions throughout the ages, weaving has been considered a part of the pejorative canon of women's work. In just about every civilization since its conception, weaving was often done by women in solitude or collaborative groups. Historically, the division of labor in most hunter-gatherer societies charged women with the domestic tasks of weaving, cooking and childcare, while men fulfilled more dangerous responsibilities associated with hunting. Through this lens, the history of weaving is, by and large, a history of women.

Woven cloth is fundamentally comprised of two interlacing sets of thread positioned horizontally and vertically. The vertical threads are known as the "warp," while horizontal threads are called the "weft." Although the basic plain weave structure of interwoven warp and weft has remained unchanged throughout millennia, technological innovations in fiber processing—from the development of simple machines to complex motorized looms—have drastically altered the appearance, utilization and social implications of woven textiles.

The first innovations in ancient woven textiles were dependent upon the invention of spun thread. However, many scientists believe that weaving predates spinning in the form of basketry. Some archaeologists have theorized that the first iterations of spinning were developed due to the tensile strength of twining, a basket weaving technique wherein two strands of bark or reed cross another as they are woven.

Heddles—the integral part of a loom used to separate and control the warp yarns.

PHOTOGRAPHY: Morgan Hale

Weaving requires the use of a loom, which holds spun threads under tension as they are woven. In its most rudimentary form, a loom is comprised of two beams upon which the warp is stretched. While weft threads may be manually woven with a needle, the innovation of using sticks or bars holding string heddles (small loops tied around alternating warp threads) made hand weaving a much more efficient process. Throughout prehistory, looms were often outfitted with two heddle bars attached to alternating warp threads to create "sheds" in the warp through which the weft was quickly passed. The invention of heddles is perhaps the most important innovation of hand weaving.

There are many different types of historic looms, including backstrap looms, handlooms and draw looms. One of the earliest types is the warp-weighted loom, which is a large, upright frame structure with weights tied to the ends of the warp to keep them taut. Warp-weighted looms have been used all over the world by many civilizations, from Minoan Cretes to the Vikings to the indigenous peoples of the Americas. They allowed for the creation of detailed, large-scale textiles, which paved the way for later innovations in tapestry weaving.

Traditionally created using a plain-weave structure, tapestry weaving is a form of pictorial weaving, which varies among cultures. The motifs found in ancient tapestries are highly symbolic, often serving as narrative pictographs in much the same way as cave paintings or petroglyphs. For example, the symbolic compositions of many ancient Turkish kilims can be read much the same way as logographic scripts, such as Egyptian hieroglyphics or Sumerian cuneiform. Symbolic pictorial motifs were also notably used in ancient Andean and Southeast Asian backstrap weaving.

Throughout the world, innovations in materials and technology allowed tapestry weaving to become highly detailed. In many ancient cultures, these weavings were used for a variety of political and spiritual purposes. In ancient China, silk Kesi tapestries became symbols of political and economic status, while Andean tapestries of the Chancay culture were ceremonially used for their magical and spiritual properties. The Akan empire in Ghana developed Kente cloth using a method called strip-weave, wherein long strips were woven and sewn together to create larger textiles. In the early 14th century, Germany and Switzerland witnessed the popularization of large, painterly tapestries. The production of elaborate hand-woven tapestries flourished across the globe, imbued with the spirit, style and history of vastly diverse regions and civilizations.

This all changed during the Industrial Revolution with the invention of the flying shuttle in 1733 and the power loom in 1784. Industrial weaving became fully automatic in 1895 with the release of the Northrop Loom, which had a self-threading shuttle holding an open-ended bobbin called a pirn. Whenever a pirn ran out of thread, the Northrop Loom had a mechanism that would automatically eject the empty pirn and load the shuttle with a fresh one. Traditional hand-weaving workshops in many areas of the world swiftly declined as a result.

However, hand-weaving practices persisted in some rural regions as hand-woven textiles became prized for their intensive labor and characteristically unique designs. Today, hand weaving is witnessing a resurgence as artists and craftspeople around the world turn away from industrially mass-produced textiles and summon the techniques, traditions and origins of weaving.

Evee Erb
Textile Artist
eveeerb.com

Introduction of Anni Albers

Anni Albers (1899-1994) was a German-born American textile artist, teacher and printmaker who bridged the divide between traditional craft and art through weaving. She was born Annelise Else Frieda Fleischmann in an affluent household in Berlin, Germany. During her childhood, she was fascinated by art and the visual world, and studied drawing and painting under the encouragement of her parents. Even though she lived a comfortable life, she eventually decided to be an artist and went to the art school in Weimar where the living conditions were harsh.

Anni attended the Bauhaus, the pioneering art school, and, in 1992, met Josef Albers. At that time, women were prohibited from studying certain disciplines. Unable to get into a glass workshop with Josef, Anni entered the weaving workshop and soon explored the possibilities of textiles.

Even though Anni preferred wall painting, after communicating with the remarkable group of women weavers, she developed an interest in weaving and began to explore it. She found the very limited and disciplined craft required her to innovate and break though the inherent form. She learned that textiles are used not just for decoration but materials, tools and everything around us.

Weaving materials.
PHOTOGRAPHY: Panayiotis Mina

In 1925, Anni and Josef were married. In the same year, the couple was sent to Dessau to teach. During that time, Anni experimented with new materials for weaving. She utilized both traditional and industrial materials in weaving, including jute, paper, horse hair, cellophane, etc. She created abstract wall hangings called "pictorial weavings" that she wanted to be read as artworks like paintings. At the same time, prompted by the new focus on production, she also created many functional textiles such as fabrics or rugs that combined the properties of durability, anti-wrinkle, sound absorption and light reflection. Her works propel the reconsideration of textiles as both an art form and functional products.

In 1928, after Walter Gropius, the founder of the Bauhaus, left Dessau, Anni and Josef moved into the teaching quarters next to Paul Klee and Wassily Kandinsky, the founding fathers of classical modernism, and began their lifelong habit of traveling. Travel became their source of inspiration. They became famous collectors who brought back art works from around the world every time they traveled.

In 1932, under the pressure from the Nazi regime, the Bauhaus moved to Berlin and operated for 10 months without further interference from the Nazi Party before permanently closing in 1933. After the close of the Bauhaus and to escape the rise of Nazism, the couple left Germany for the United States where they were invited to teach at the experimental Black Mountain College in North Carolina. During their years teaching at Black Mountain, Anni continued to create extraordinary weavings and showed her weavings around the U.S. Meanwhile, the couple frequently traveled to Mexico, exploring and collecting the work of the Latin American weavers. The unique weaving techniques and style of the work of the Latin American weavers had a great impact on Anni's late weaving style. She was the first textile artist to hold a personal exhibition at the Museum of Modern Art in New York, which helped establish her as one of the most well-known weavers of the day. She learned how to use backstrap looms, some of the very earliest looms, and taught her students the techniques she had acquired during the trips.

In 1949, Anni and Josef left Black Mountain and moved to Connecticut. After leaving Black Mountain, Anni was still committed to education and spent years working on mass-produced patterns, creating "pictorial weavings" and writing. In 1963, she started printmaking. In 1965, she published her seminal text, *On Weaving*, which served as a powerful voice of the mid-century textile design movement in the United States. Her in-depth study of textiles and analysis of design theories influenced the history of craftsmanship and advanced the position of design. In 1971, the couple founded the Josef and Anni Albers Foundation, a nonprofit organization dedicated to preserving and promoting their aesthetic and philosophical principles.

After the death of Josef, Anni continued to expand her textile and printmaking and had several exhibitions. She also received lifetime achievement awards during this time.

Throughout her lifetime, she explored textiles as a means of expression and experimentation. Her study on the practicality of textiles and the functionally unique textiles has had a far-reaching impact on many textile artists. Anni Albers died in 1994.

A weaving loom.
PHOTOGRAPHY: Rie Endo

List of Multiple Weaving Materials

Weaving is a technique in which a linear or strip-shaped material, principally yarn, is repeatedly overlapped to form flat or three-dimensional weaving. Weavers or textile artists choose their materials according to their needs and the visual effect they want to create. The use of different materials can bring different outcomes. Weavings like cotton and silk can bring feelings of softness and comfort, while sisal is stiff and durable and can be used to make receptacles. While choosing, they also explore some surprising materials which can also be used to weave. Here is a list of fibers commonly used in weaving.

Animal Fibers

Animal fibers are mainly hair, fur, wool, feathers or silk from animals. They are one of the natural fibers widely used in the manufacturing world.

Silk: Silk is a natural fiber mainly obtained from cocoons and spiders. Mulberry silk is made from cocoons. The fully-grown silkworm that eats mulberry leaves will spin a cocoon that is made with a sticky substance. This substance is the mixture of fibroin protein compounds and sericin, the silk gum. When this sticky substance comes in contact with air, it will solidify into the silk fiber. Silk is the strongest natural fiber. It is tough and highly elastic. It is characterized by being super-absorbent, heat retaining and easily stained. Silk is mostly used to weave garments, tapestries, rugs and clothes.

Alpaca: Alpaca is a kind of wool obtained from alpaca sheep. Compared with regular sheep's wool, it is warmer and lighter, softer and glossier. The colors of alpaca are mostly white, gray, reddish brown and black. It can be used to make various products.

Mohair: Mohair is derived from the hair of the North African Angora goat. Mohair has a beautiful nickname, "diamond fiber," for its high luster and sheen. Blending mohair with other fibers can keep the qualities of the textile. Mohair can be easily dyed and it can be used to make hats, sweaters and other fluffy accessories.

Mohair being used to make soft thread.
PHOTOGRAPHY: The Ninevites

Plant Fibers

Plant fibers are cellulose-based materials for weaving. They are divided into three types: seed fibers, bast fibers and hard fibers. Seed fibers are harvested from seeds or seed pods of plants like cotton. Bast fibers are obtained from inner bark or stems of plants. And hard fibers, also named leaf fibers, are collected from the leaves of the plants.

Cotton: Cotton is a kind of plant fiber that is soft and fluffy. It is produced from a cotton plant that loses its flowers, leaving behind a large cotton boll containing the white and downy cotton. Cotton is a soft and breathable fiber that can hold up to 27 times its weight in water. It is mostly spun into yarn or thread to make comfortable textiles.

Bamboo: Bamboo grows very fast. It is a traditional weaving material in Asia. Bamboo can be easily split into strips and threads, which are the basic materials for weaving. Bamboo strips are smooth and stiff. The crafts made from bamboo are waterproof and durable.

Grass: Grass is widely used in weaving goods like baskets, hats and bags. Many kinds of grasses can be used to weave. For example, rush and straw are commonly used in weaving. Usually, people harvest the grasses, wash them and then dry them in the sun. After finishing, the grass will become resilient and can be dyed, and used to weave.

People harvesting rush grasses.
PHOTOGRAPHY: Taiwan Yuan-Li Handiwork Association

Rattan: Rattan is a climbing palm with long, tough stems that mostly grows in Indonesia. It is also one of the fastest-growing plant fibers and can regenerate in five to seven years. Characterized by its strong, bendable and durable qualities, rattan is often used as wood to make baskets and furniture but it also can be used to make clothes that resist heat, cold, moisture and temperature fluctuations.

Sisal: Sisal is a hard fiber taken from the leaves of sisal plants, which can survive in hot and dry areas. Being capable of enduring the hard environment, the sisal fiber is coarse, strong and durable. It also has the ability to stretch. With good insulation properties and because it's highly resistant to bacterial damage, the sisal fiber is mostly used for rope and twine. It can also be used to make paper, clothes, hats, etc.

Rare Fiber

Besides the commonly used fibers, there are more materials that can be applied to weaving.

Nylon: Nylon is a kind of synthetic textile, invented in 1931 by an organic chemist named Wallace Hume Carothers. It is a thermoplastic material that can be melted and developed into fiber. It is a fiber that imitates silk. Nylon has a lot of good qualities. It is resilient, durable, lightweight, lustrous, easily dyed, etc. With these good qualities, nylon is widely used in producing pantyhose, dresses, socks, hats, carpets and so on.

Wire: Wire is a new material for weaving. Different types of wires can be used for weaving: fine silver, sterling silver, copper, brass and coated wire. Some wires are soft and easily shaped, while others are strong and hard and serve as the base. Wire is mostly used for making jewelry.

Glass fiber: Glass fiber is a man-made fiber made from extremely fine fibers of glass. It is tensile, less brittle and heat-proof. In 1893, Edward Drummond Libbey exhibited a glass dress woven by combing glass fibers and silk threads. Even though the dress was spectacular, it was practically valueless because the glass fiber is too stiff to be worn. Glass fibers are mostly used to make home furnishings.

Copper being patinated in fire.
PHOTOGRAPHY: Sally Blake

PHOTOGRAPHY: **Reni van den Brandt (photos on page 016–017).**

Hermine Van Dijck | Belgium

· Hermine Van Dijck ·

Hermine Van Dijck is a Belgian textile designer. She attended the Ghent School of Art where she specialized in textile design and graduated in 2012. Later, she was awarded an internship at a weaving company based in Paris where she developed her interest in weaving even more. During this experience, she realized that designing fabrics for fashion wasn't what she was dreaming about and that the speed of the fashion industry was too quick for what she wanted to create. She wanted to create pieces for the home, preferably all hand-woven and unique. She wanted to make creations that could last a lifetime. Also, she prefers weaving what she feels and sees, rather than weaving for a boss and someone else's inspiration.

In 2013, Hermine opened her own studio in Antwerp, Belgium where she works on hand-woven designs and interesting collaborations. Her work is characterized by the use of color as the most important thing within her designs. Her love for hand-woven imperfections and geometrical patterns are unmistakably hers.

Hermine translates poetic feelings into strong visual designs. By using unique graphic combinations and natural fibers, she is inspired by weaving on her Scandinavian looms, the atmosphere of the high north and traditional textiles. She cleverly combines the artisanal character of old weaving techniques with modern aesthetics into textiles for the home and heart.

1. Please share with us your weaving process from conception to creation.

I mostly start with a mood board where I work around a certain theme. I search for pictures that have nice colors, objects with lovely textures, images with great atmospheres, etc. This research is the start of a collection. After some research time, I have to stop myself from doing more research because it can be a never-ending process and sometimes it can also be confusing seeing other people's images and works. After the research is over, I start working on a gut feeling and I try not to think too much. It usually comes together very naturally, although I also have my bad days, like any other designers. I always start making samples very impulsively and using different techniques like knitting, drawing, photography, weaving, silk screening, tufting, embroidering and so on. These samples will be the beginning of a new collection—they're like the first words of a story. After a little time playing with the samples, I try to put everything together in order to make bigger pieces, which can then become a product.

2. Would you please share the story of your Scandinavian weaving looms?

I have several weaving looms and weaving frames in my workspace. Most of the time, I use my little wooden weaving loom, which was made by a woodworker in Antwerp. He makes them in a small woodworking shop in his home. It's an honor to be able to weave on a loom made in Antwerp. It's rather small, but perfect for experimenting. My other loom is a bit bigger and uses pedals to move the shafts of the loom. I bought this Toika loom from a textile school in The Netherlands. The loom was made in Finland and is decades old. I use this loom to make bigger pieces and little collections, such as the cushion collection that I recently made or the woven wall hangings.

3. You also create products according to customers' demands. Do you negotiate with your customers to ensure the outcome is satisfying for both of you?

PHOTOGRAPHY: **Reni van den Brandt (photos on page 018–019).**

Weaving process.

I do make pieces on demand for customers. I will first meet the customers in my workspace to discuss their wishes. I will also explain to them how I work and how the process of designing and weaving a piece works. We discuss their preference for colors, textures and sizes. Often customers come to me for my personal use of colors and very often they give me enough freedom to create their piece. Mostly, I first make a small sample before making the final piece, so the customers can imagine how their piece will look. I've made several scarves for weddings, cushions to fit customers' interiors, etc. The outcome is always very interesting. However, I do feel like I only can make custom-made pieces that have similar aesthetics to my personal work. Hand-waving is a very time consuming craft and I would feel sad to work a long time on a design that I don't like. That's why sometimes I don't accept new jobs because they don't fit my personal style.

4. Most of your works are inspired by Bauhaus weavings? Could you tell us a little bit about Bauhaus weavings? What did you learn from Bauhaus weavings?

Bauhaus was a turning point for every female weaver. It took hand weaving out of the box called "women's work," and moved it to its rightful place alongside art, design and architecture. For a very long time, I've been inspired by the Bauhaus movement and especially by Anni Albers. Her designs are an exquisite example of the power of hand weaves. The beautiful graphics that are known for the play with lines and blocks, the technical knowledge about double weaves and the beautiful use of fibers make her work special. She once said that a weave will define itself while being woven. It can be an artwork or a useful product. That's a very interesting thing because this is how it often works for myself, as well. Big decisions about the weave will be made when I'm behind my loom. I'm also very inspired by the aesthetics they used in their work and I'm very attracted to geometrical shapes like blocks, lines, and triangles. Even though my color choices are very different from the Bauhaus weavers, I believe there is a connection between our aesthetics and feelings about weaving.

5. Besides weaving, do you have other hobbies or passions?

Yes, I do. I love yarn, in general. So I adore knitting and doing embroidery works. It's the most incredible feeling to work on a hand-knit cardigan for weeks and then keep yourself warm with your handmade piece during the cold winter days. I also recently started ceramics school. Even though it's a completely new material, it has similarities to weaving. It demands patience from its maker and is very focused on technique, too. I love to feel the earth in my hand. And I love to create things with an unfamiliar material.

PHOTOGRAPHY: **Eefje de Coninck (bottom photo on page 020).**

The Blush Scarf

"The Blush Scarf" is a collection of hand-woven scarves woven on a 16-shaft table loom made by a local woodworker in Antwerp. This collection is inspired by the colors of spring flowers.

Tools: 16-shaft table loom
Materials: wool, merino, cashmere, cotton

PHOTOGRAPHY: **Eefje de Coninck (photo on page 022).**

› Pupuce Potholders and Cushion

"Pupuce" is a collection of hand-woven potholders and cushions made on an eight-shaft counterbalance loom. It is inspired by Bauhaus weavings and based on a play with colors and structures. The name "Pupuce" is in memory of Hermine Van Dijck's sweet 18-year-old cat that disappeared suddenly in 2017.

Tools: eight-shaft countermarch loom
Materials: wool, cotton

PHOTOGRAPHY: **Eefje de Coninck (photos on page 024–025).**

Ping Ping Blanket

"Ping Ping Blanket" is a collection of baby blankets woven on an eight-shaft hand loom inspired by Bauhaus weavings.

Tools: eight-shaft countermarch loom by Toika
Materials: wool and cotton lining

"The magic about weaving is that there are a lot of different components that influence the process: the colors, the yarn, the pattern, the calculation, etc. Every little detail can change the resulting fabric completely."

Studio Nom | The Netherlands

· Nompumelelo ·

Studio Nom was founded by Nompumelelo, a fiber and textile artist based in Alkmaar, The Netherlands. Having mastered the traditional techniques of weaving and macramé, she translates these techniques into contemporary designs. After working in the field of design for years, she decided to take the leap and embark on her creative exploration—weaving. Armed with all her scraps of yarn from her crochet adventures and some old weaving books, she got started.

"I love the endless possibilities weaving brings, diversity of techniques, playing with colors and different yarns or fabrics," says Nompumelelo. "For me, weaving is all about experimenting, which made it the perfect playground to find my way."

In 2013, Nompumelelo started her business called "nom vol van kleur," which means "full of color." In 2017, she changed the name to "Studio Nom" to cover all kinds of artworks she has done and could do in the future. The studio is, in fact, one of the smallest rooms in her house, but it is packed with yarn, rope, wood, unfinished projects and great ideas. A lot of projects started there including her GEO series. Now, Nompumelelo also works as a freelance do-it-yourself stylist for a Dutch magazine, which means more creations will come from this small room. She enjoys working at home because when she steps out of her studio, she can immediately embrace her family life—her cat is chasing his tail, her girls are doing homework or playing games, and, on some days, her husband is preparing a home-cooked meal.

1. Please share with us your daily working schedule.

As I work from my home, I can skip the commute, so after my family eats breakfast and I see the kids off to school, I can jump in straight away. I would love to say my whole day is all about creating and working out new designs, but running a small business means a whole lot more. I'm the designer and the helpdesk support and any other roles you can think of in between. And that doesn't mean I have all those necessary skills. So, I'm learning as I go. That said, I have never been happier with what I do! I don't have any pieces in stock, so every wall hanging is made especially for the customer, which also keeps me flexible to make a custom order. I love receiving an order in which the customers clarify where they want to put the piece of artwork. Days are spent answering emails, packing, shipping and on my social media presence. But, luckily, most days are spent on making pieces while binge-listening to podcasts.

2. Both crochet and weaving are textile art forms and you tried both of them. How do you think they're different?

I really loved crocheting and found it to be relaxing. It almost felt like saying mantras. I only used one or two stitches over and over again. But, at the same time, I found crocheting restrictive as the playground it offered me is way too small. Weaving opened up so many possibilities for me. It's so much easier to think outside the box. I hosted a weaving workshop for kids at school some years ago. The kids picked up the one-up-one-down weave in a flash, so we started to weave vertical lines. A boy in my class didn't get it and came up with a piece that I still don't understand, but it looked fantastic! That's what I love about weaving. It gives room for experimentation.

3. Please share with us your working process for the GEO series.

Creating a new design always means undergoing a series of processes. In the beginning, I looked at basic weaving

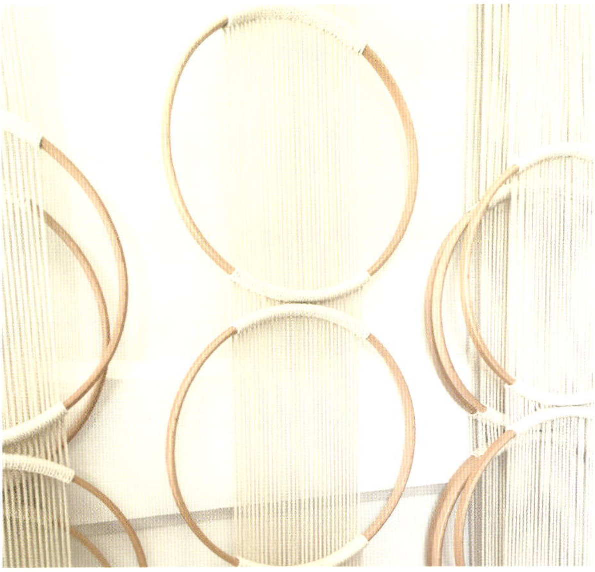

patterns, like a plain weave, twill and a honeycomb weave. I was especially interested in the part that normally would be repeated and took it from there. But I also love the geometric patterns you can find in a diversity of cultures around the world and in Art Deco design. Inspiration is everywhere. For me, there's always an idea in my mind, but I never know where it will take me. People often ask me if I make a sketch first. But I never do. I always jump right in, step back, look and look again. There are a lot of do-overs, but that's also a part of the process.

4. Please talk about the fibers you've tried. How did you find the most suitable fiber for your work?

When I started out weaving, I mostly worked with all the yarn I had stocked up during my crocheting days: cottons and wool. I added roving, searched for vintage yarn, cut up old jeans or everything I found suitable. I was mostly looking for structure. But as my weavings changed, I started to have other wishes. I needed my yarn to be much stronger because I pull every warp and weft really tight. It couldn't be slippery as all the knots need to hold. I wanted it to unravel easily, but not too easily. Finally, I ended up with a clean and natural look. As I mentioned, I also did some macramé. I used cotton rope, which has all the qualities I was looking for, so using my macramé rope for my weavings seems to be the perfect match.

5. Now, you are concentrating on the GEO series, which quite separates itself from other forms of weaving. How did you find your personal style in the weaving world?

You have to practice as much as you can and, along the way, you'll find the part you love the most. When learning a new technique, it is very tempting to put everything you know in one design. As my knowledge and confidence grew, I got more and more comfortable leaving things out. That is where my GEO wall hangings started to take shape. I always love the way a weaving looks while it's still on the loom. With the tension on the warp, the lines look very clean. After some research, I stumbled on the embroidery hoop which I had laying around. With a macramé knot, I secured my warp and I was ready to go.

6. What has been your greatest challenge to date? How did you conquer it?

My greatest challenge would absolutely be to grow more confident in my work. Even though I have always been creating as a fashion designer, a do-it-yourself stylist or a designer with my collection, I still have the first urge to hideaway. For almost every step I take on this journey, I have to give myself a pep talk. Showing your work is showing a part of you, and the world outside your studio can be scary. When my customers purchase my work, I always send them a note: "Your purchase made me do a little dance! And I hope you'll dance with me." And I really do a happy dance. I'm so honored if someone tells me they saved up to buy one of my pieces.

GEO-04

"GEO-04" is Nompumelelo's first handmade wall hanging from the GEO series, made in 2018. She attempted to focus on the weaving design and keeping the weaving in its frame.

Tools: scissors, flat-nose pliers, hands
Materials: beech wood rings and dowel, 100% cotton rope

GEO-3

"GEO-3" is another experiment in adding circles and colors.

Tools: scissors, flat-nose pliers, hands
Materials: beech wood rings and dowel, 100% cotton rope (white and brick)

Rie Endo | Japan

· **Rie Endo** ·

Rie Endo was born in Japan in 1982. She loved to draw since childhood and she studied art and fashion for a long time. While studying textiles, she developed a great interest in a Japanese loom manufacturer. She then set up her workshop, Rocca, and devoted herself to weaving. Now, all the work of dyeing yarn, weaving and tailoring is done by her. The finished fabric is so soft that it cannot be replaced by mechanical weaving. One can sometimes feel the warmth of the work from the texture of her weavings. Since ancient times, people have woven clothes and worn them. As time goes by, people are more focused on productivity and efficiency. She believes that weavings are more about colors, patterns and the people who wear them and she respects the simple act of weaving each one carefully.

1. Could you please tell us a little bit about your brand, Rocca? What was the most challenging aspect of launching Rocca? Could you please share some stories about your workplace?

Rocca is my weaving workshop. I built a house with a space for the workshop two years ago. When I designed the house, I thought the workshop should be bright and with good view. So, I took the environment into consideration. There were some challenges while launching Rocca. The biggest challenge was finding a large hand loom because in Japan they're not readily available, and they're very valuable and expensive.

2. You dye the yarn yourself. Do you use natural dyes or others? What do you need to pay attention to during the process?

I prefer using chemical dyes, rather than natural dyes. When dyeing, I need to pay maximum attention to temperature and time, so as not to damage the yarn. After I make the fabric, I use it to create clothing. I believe that the soul and beauty of the product are in the details. While sewing, I need to pay the most attention to the parts that cannot be clearly seen.

3. Please share with us your weaving process from conception to creation and tell us a bit about your chosen techniques and how you use them.

Before weaving, I will decide on the color and dye the yarn according to the season. When weaving is completed, I use the material to sew bags and shawls. I sometimes sew by hand or use a sewing machine. For example, I will apply different techniques to make a custom-made suit. Once you start, it can never be changed. You should be very careful and the process is time-consuming.

Rie Endo paints and matches the color on paper before dyeing the clothes.

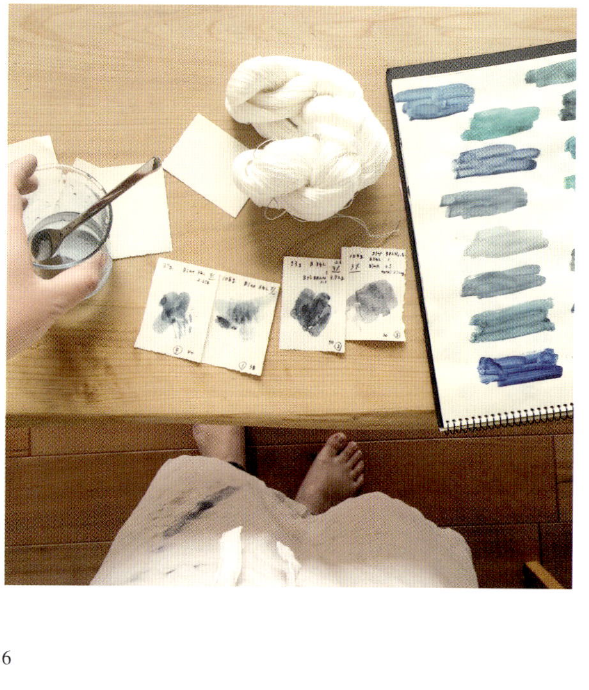

4. The patterns of your works are neat and the style of your works is simple and elegant. How do you get inspiration and how do you achieve this style?

Yes, my works are mostly classical and simple. I usually get inspiration from classic movies, art books and architecture. The way to achieve this style is to keep my house simple and comfortable. I want to draw and weave with a natural look. A quality and simple life makes people happy.

5. We noticed that you use paint and match the color on paper before dyeing. Does the outcome sometimes not match what you expect? What has been your greatest challenge to date? How did you conquer it?

I used to have trouble with colors, but I've improved with experience. However, I still feel it is difficult to dye gray. Lightness is very important. The technique of using delicate yarn is necessary, so I practiced a lot.

Simple Weave

"Simple Weave" is a simple and sophisticated design that will not be obsolete even when the times change.

Materials: linen, silk

Bird's Eye and Herringbone.

Alinea

Rie Endo imagined the symbol alinéa, which is the indention when going to a new paragraph, then designed the pattern. It is an image of dividing and going forward forever.

Materials: silk, linen

Julia Astreou | Cyprus

· **Julia Astreou** ·

Julia Astreou is an artist, researcher and textile designer specializing in woven textiles based in Nicosia, Cyprus. She has a bachelor's degree in textiles and fashion design from the Winchester School of Art in the United Kingdom. Julia went on to complete a structure, material and color course at the National Superior School of Fine Arts of Paris to broaden her understanding of art and textiles.

She worked at Cyprus Handicraft Service for 21 years and has done extensive research on Cypriot textiles. Julia was the textiles adviser for two films (*Weaving Ladies of Cyprus* and *Lefkara Lace*) on traditional Cypriot weaving and Lefkara lace. Her enthusiasm for traditional Cypriot textiles led to the creation of the Cyprus Textile Route website and booklet in cooperation with the European Textiles Network.

Julia has also had solo painting exhibitions in Nicosia and has represented Cyprus at renowned textile art exhibitions in Europe, including the International Tapestry Triennial in Lodz, Poland and La Borsa Accessorio Necessario in Florence, and Turin, Italy and Antwerp, Belgium. She has also created theatrical costumes for the Epidavros Festival in Greece through the Cyprus National Theatrical Organization. In 2010, she was awarded a silver medal from the Sciences, Arts and Letters organization in Paris for her work in textile art and design as well as her research into traditional textiles.

1. How do you get inspiration and transform your thoughts into the various patterns?

Usually, I get inspired by my experiences and interests. The "Arete" shawls are inspired by Queen Arete's costume, which I designed and wove for the theatrical production *The Odyssey*. The design is based on drawings from the pottery of the fifth century BC depicting the characters from *The Odyssey*. Its cotton warp is left unwoven at regular intervals giving unexpected shapes when parts of the shawl overlap.

The schemata cushion covers contain patterns which suggest symbols and diagrams of abstract concepts. Despite their simplicity, they can be seen as linear representations of complex theories. These theories, however, are characterized by notions existing in balance.

The "Rhythm" cushion covers are inspired by rhythmic patterns. The variation of the shapes may show a differentiation in the beat, which results in a harmonious musical piece as well as a harmonious visual pattern.

The "Rhythm" design is linked to a woven wall hanging I made to represent Cyprus in 2011 at an exhibition in Kaunas, Lithuania during the 16th European Textile Network Conference.

2. We noticed that you have done extensive research on Cypriot traditional textiles. What drove you to do the research?

It is important to study traditional textiles as they are valuable sources of inspiration for the creation of contemporary articles. They are full of the knowledge and the wisdom that passed from generation to generation. Research is also important because traditional textiles lead back to history. Often research reveals historical facts that influenced and reformed traditional textiles. The old weavers and embroiderers who are still alive today lived in an age with a different social, political and economic structure. Their lives were more difficult than today as many had to help their husbands with agricultural work, look after the family as well as do their weaving,

embroidery or lace work. Sometimes their work was the main source of income for the family. Many are very talented, kind, hospitable and deeply religious artisans. This world is sadly reaching an end. I believe it is my duty to record this information as it will be soon lost.

3. You previously worked at the Cyprus Handicraft Service. Could you please tell us a little bit about it? What was your most memorable experience?

The Cyprus Handicraft Service is part of the Ministry of Energy Commerce and Industry. It was created in 1978 and one of its main aims was to offer employment to the Greek Cypriot refugees who had to leave the north of the island after the Turkish invasion of 1974. Other important aims of the service were to study, preserve and retain the local handicrafts. I worked there for 21 years and I was responsible for the embroidery and weaving sections.

My most memorable experience was when we provided help for the weavers in the villages situated on the far western side of the island near the beautiful Akamas peninsula. Life in those remote villages was very different than in the town centers. We had to gain the trust of the weavers who were cautious of any strangers contacting their villages.

4. You have used some traditional looms to weave. Which traditional loom do you like best? Why?

Nowadays, there are two types of traditional Cypriot looms one can use. The type I prefer to use is quite big. The warp on this loom is stretched from the front beam around the back beam and hangs in a ball over the head of the weaver. I prefer to use this type of loom where the warp has a long stretch and, for this reason, it has even tension. I also find the way to place the warp on the loom easy. In the second type of loom, which is used in the Paphos area on the western side of the island, the warp is wound around the back beam by using special loom implements. I find this procedure more complicated to use. The winding of the warp around the back beam is similar to Greek and most European looms.

5. What advice would you like to give to an aspiring textile artist?

I believe that an aspiring artist should work hard and find their strong points in designing. Even if their breadwinning job is not satisfying, they should always carry on with their work. I believe the two most important values in life are work and love. Progress is another quality that is very important and relates to the first two. So, if artists work hard and make the correct choices for their designs, there will come a time when their work will be appreciated and distinguished.

‹ Asproploumia Lampshade

Hand-woven lampshade based on Cypriot traditional "asproploumia" fabrics.

Tools: Cypriot traditional loom
Materials: cotton, cane, sisal

ˆ Schemata Series

All "Schemata" series cushion covers are woven with black and red yarn against a contrasting, natural-colored cotton background. These colors were also used in early traditional textiles. Weaving the geometric patterns involves a lot of counting warp threads and placing yarn by hand.

Tools: Cypriot traditional loom
Materials: cotton

Arete Shawls

Hand-woven white "Arete" shawl with textured stripes. Its cotton warp is left unwoven and interlaced in net-like structures. Unexpected shapes result when the shawl is worn around the body and parts of it overlap. It reminds one of sea anemones and tropical flowers. The shawl was inspired by Queen Arete's costume, which Julia designed and wove for the theatrical production of *The Odyssey* performed at a Cypria festival. The design is based on drawings from pottery of the fifth century BC depicting the characters of *The Odyssey*.

Tools: traditional Cypriot loom
Materials: cotton, wool, rayon

Sarah Neubert | America

· Sarah Neubert ·

Sarah Neubert is a fiber artist who lives in Fort Collins, Colorado. She uses her works to explore the complexities of everyday life and the hidden patterns in the natural world. Sarah sees weaving as a meditative collaboration between her and the raw, organic and unexpected materials she chooses. Every piece she makes is a search for balance, self-knowledge and a deeper connection to our sweet Mother Earth. Sarah is also a weaving teacher. As a weaving teacher, she seeks to impart to her students a sense of curiosity and adventure as they begin to explore the limitless possibilities within the world of fibers.

1. Your works remind us of the boundless wilderness. Is that the feeling you want to pass to your audience? What do you want to express through your work?

I am very interested in exploring the human connection to the natural world, especially in a culture that has largely lost sight of that connection. A major element of my work is a search for my place in the rhythms and cycles of the earth. Weaving itself is one of the oldest crafts in the archaeological record and has always been a collaboration with nature—taking things that grow on the earth and using them to weave coverings for the body, vessels for holding food and ceremonial items used in rituals to deepen our understanding of our relationship to nature. It's a rhythmic, meditative craft that serves as a beautiful metaphor for the way we are all connected and to the fragile planet that sustains us.

I hope my work gives audiences a sense of grounding. I hope they are reminded that we are small parts of a huge, interconnected whole. Each of us belongs, and, although we may not feel like it at times, the smallest work of our hands makes a difference to the fabric of our world. If my weavings encourage people to try to understand their place in the fabric, then I've done my job.

2. You live at the foot of the Rocky Mountains. Do you collect textile materials yourself? How do you find the most suitable fibers for your works?

When I started weaving, it was a huge challenge to find the right fibers and yarns. I discovered early on that I'm attracted to materials in their raw state. Minimally processed fiber is better for the environment and it's more suitable to the organic, textural feel of my work. It took a lot of research and help from fiber friends to find sources for the yarns I use now.

I also purchase a lot of my materials second-hand, from Craigslist, eBay and estate sales. I love finding unusual things to weave with. It contributes to the element of surprise in my work and means that many of my pieces can never be re-created because they were made with a material I can't get again. I sometimes forage for materials in nature—pine needles, grasses, seedpods and tree bark are readily available and I love the unexpected ways they behave in a weaving.

3. We noticed that most of your works are woven by combining different materials like cotton, wool, bamboo, brass and so on.

PHOTOGRAPHY: **Caleb Young (photos on page 052–053).**

Is it difficult to weave with different materials? Will different materials affect the outcome of your works?

One of the most enjoyable parts of my process is learning how to work with unusual materials. It's a process of discovery and collaboration. Raw hemp behaves differently than raw linen. Silk behaves differently than wool. And, of course, whenever I introduce a non-fiber element such as wood or metal, I end up with unexpected challenges—but it's a wonderfully tactile, spontaneous way to work. I try to be an open channel, truly working with my materials rather than bending them to my will. It's part of the spontaneity and surprise. Of course, sometimes I will try new material and will be unsuccessful in the first few tries. But that makes it all the more satisfying when I finally discover the technique or combination of materials that creates a new, exciting work of art.

4. Please tell us a bit about your chosen techniques and how you use them.

I mostly use plain weave as my basic structure and then employ a variety of techniques, such as soumak, rya knots or overshot to create surface interest in parts of the piece. I use tapestry techniques when making shapes or blending colors and I even dip into some basketry and knot-tying techniques from time to time. Most of my weaving is done on my larger tapestry looms, so I can see the entire piece as I work, but I also use my floor looms when appropriate. Because my materials vary so widely from one piece to the next, I have to be versatile and willing to adopt new techniques. The beautiful thing about weaving is that it's been around for thousands of years and used in so many different applications that there is always something to draw from and adapt to my work and style.

5. What other hobbies or passions do you have besides weaving?

I write music and play in a band. Music is a different outlet for me because it creates a special connection between the performer and the audience, and I find it fascinating that songs impact me in new ways every time I play them. When weaving is finished, it's finished—but a song can keep evolving.

I am also very interested in neuroscience and the way our bodies process trauma. I am looking into ways to combine my love of weaving and the deep impact that somatic (body-based) therapy has had on my life. I would love to develop a modality for people to use weaving as a healing tool, a way to get into the body and gently restore our mental health. It's not a unique idea, but I think it's an under-used one and something I've been pondering for a few years now. The human nervous system is boundlessly fascinating and I hope to deepen my understanding of how working with our hands can help us to heal ourselves and become more resilient, regulated beings.

PHOTOGRAPHY: **Caleb Young (photo on page 054, upper photos on page 055). Urban Oak Photography (bottom photo on page 055)**

‹ Descent

This commissioned work was inspired by organic textures and vintage Ikat prints, drawing color inspiration from the client's existing decor.

Tools: frame loom, beater comb
Materials: wool warp, vintage and second-hand wool weft

˄ Window Installation

A series of four panels created in collaboration with Wander Designs of Austin, Texas. Sarah wove the panels as a narrative series with each piece flowing into the next. The pieces were then installed as window treatments in a bohemian-inspired dining room.

Tools: frame loom, tapestry needle, shed stick, beating comb
Materials: wool warp, vintage and second-hand wool weft

PHOTOGRAPHY: **Caleb Young (photo on page 057).**

‹ Unfound Forms 1

This weaving is a meditative piece made from strips of torn fabric from the blankets her two children were wrapped in when they were born in addition to the clothes her husband and she wore to the births. Both births were difficult and traumatic for Sarah and very different from her expectations, but she found much relief and healing at the loom as she worked with these special materials.

Tools: frame loom
Materials: wool warp, fabric strips

‹ Small River

This weaving was based off a photo Sarah took of a trickle of water running down a dirt road. It reminded her of a quote about art making by Jean Rhys: "There are great rivers that feed the lake, like Tolstoy or Dostoyevsky. And then there are mere trickles, like Jean Rhys. All that matters is feeding the lake. I don't matter. The lake matters. You must keep feeding the lake."

Tools: frame loom
Materials: wool warp, deconstructed hemp rope, upholstery piping, cotton chenille

˄ Cascade Necklace

Because embodiment is something Sarah works on daily, she loves making pieces for the body. She sees them as amulets, reminders of our physical connection to the earth.

Tools: frame loom
Materials: linen, vintage cotton rug yarn

Aggeliki Dimitriadou | Greece

· **Aggeliki Dimitriadou** ·

Based in Attica, Greece, Aggeliki Dimitriadou is a self-taught textile artist. She was unconsciously inspired by her grandmother who was a weaver, too. But the weaving procedure as meditation was the real inspiration for her decision to be a weaving artist. Aggeliki always keeps learning. She uses every new method and technique as a tool to express her thoughts. She mindfully collects natural materials for her work while supporting a slow-living philosophy and getting inspired by nature. She prefers earthy colors to underline what she wants to express through her works, the relation between the natural material and its properties and the weaving as a human archetypal creation method. The natural and raw material is one of her primary inputs. She's also inspired by nature and artists from other cultures. Aggeliki also uses discarded fibers to make small project, so nothing is wasted. She believes that nothing, no material, no human labor or idea should be wasted and that wasting is an irresponsible behavior. So, on a completed large weaving piece, she not only sees the weaving piece itself, but also the new materials it produces with its leftovers. Aggeliki is still learning and will keep incorporating new ideas into her work as it continuously evolves.

1. Please share with us your weaving process from conception to creation.

Even though I approach every new project separately, most of the time it all begins from the material. It is nature that shows the way and I follow. I'm always searching for material, the texture, the colors, the weight, the thickness and other properties. You have to look closely and with great attention. After I collect samples or even entire bundles, I put them together by color, by texture and by contrast. Sometimes I make entire piles and some other times it's just with one fiber as warp and weft that weaving begins. Those material properties create links, every weft when positioned leads to a different expression and, while working, every project takes its own way. The procedure continues after weaving as pieces are stitched together or positioned in many different ways.

2. Your works are mostly woven with natural fibers. Why do you prefer using natural fibers? What's the advantage and disadvantage of natural fibers?

My works are woven only with natural fibers and that's because the natural properties of the prime material are one of the most crucial aspects of my work. The human intervention with the fibers begins in the making of the yarn. I prefer yarns that maintain as much as possible of the characteristics in raw form. Although, many times, the yarns I'm working with are naturally dyed by me or my suppliers, it's always with absolute ecological and ethical awareness. During the process from the harvest of the prime raw material to the ready yarn, I'm absolutely certain that nobody gets hurt, plant or creature, nobody is treated badly or unfairly and that nothing is wasted. There are no disadvantages regarding natural fibers if the choices are wise and ethical. In that way, we not only celebrate life through art, but we also protect our ecosystem and help people earn a decent living.

3. Please tell us a bit about your chosen techniques and how you use them.

Since I have never been systematically trained in any technique, traditional or contemporary, I consider it an

opportunity to weave free of any standard procedure. All weaving techniques have been developed to give precise properties to a fabric such as strength, weight, insulation or elasticity and they are means of expression for my work. Since I'm trying to express different things in my projects, the techniques I use vary as well as the loom types. On Saori looms, for example, unlike vertical looms, the project is wrapping up on the drum as the procedure evolves, so it cannot be seen entirely while working. That requires a different composing approach. Every technique, from the simplest to the most complex traditional weaving, is a tool of expression of the human condition as an archetypal human creation procedure.

4. You often post your weaving process on social media. What role does social media play in your artistic development?

The art of weaving that once flourished in Greece, together with other forms of folk art, have been abandoned during the last 50 or so years. This is not only a Greek phenomenon, but, all over the planet, an industrial reality has taken the place of the older and more natural world. The contemporary digital reality, a catalyst of globalization, is an extremely powerful tool to connect people around the globe. Inside this world of alienation and through this vast network, I would like my work to carry the message that slow procedures, natural materials, an ethical approach and human expression still exist. The physical world still exists and it is full of life. I have never expected that so many people would be interested in such a message. Through my social media feedback, I realized that a great number of people are interested in such a message and I am thrilled to be sharing my weaving practice with such an amazing community.

5. Would you please share the story of your Japanese Saori weaving looms?

I began working with handmade, improvised looms of different types and dimensions. I prefer to be free of the traditional techniques and of the heavy loom instrument of my childhood memories. After studying ancient and traditional weaving, I realized that the loom was, most of the time, a light and versatile instrument. In many cases, the loom as an item existed only during the weaving procedure and with the warp on. At other times, it was just a pile of sticks and rods. Nevertheless, while researching Asian cultures and weaving traditions, I encountered the Saori no mori looms and philosophy. Free weaving is an approach that's very similar to my way of thinking and also the Saori looms are very well-made, light and versatile. They are so reliable that I couldn't resist. Since then, the majority of my works have been made on Saori looms.

6. What advice would you give to an aspiring textile artist?

Without any rush, carefully look and listen inside you. Look and listen around you and feel part of this world full of life. If you feel, understand and respect, the rest will follow.

Wearable Art Clothing

Hand woven on a Saori loom, this art clothing is slow-made with natural fibers and it supports the wabisabi philosophy with their imperfections along with a dedication to the sustainable. They are made to last long with proper care.

Tools: Saori loom, Saori shuttles, yarn swift
Materials: Khadi cotton, peace silk, Eri and Tussar mixed handspun silk, mulberry silk yarn

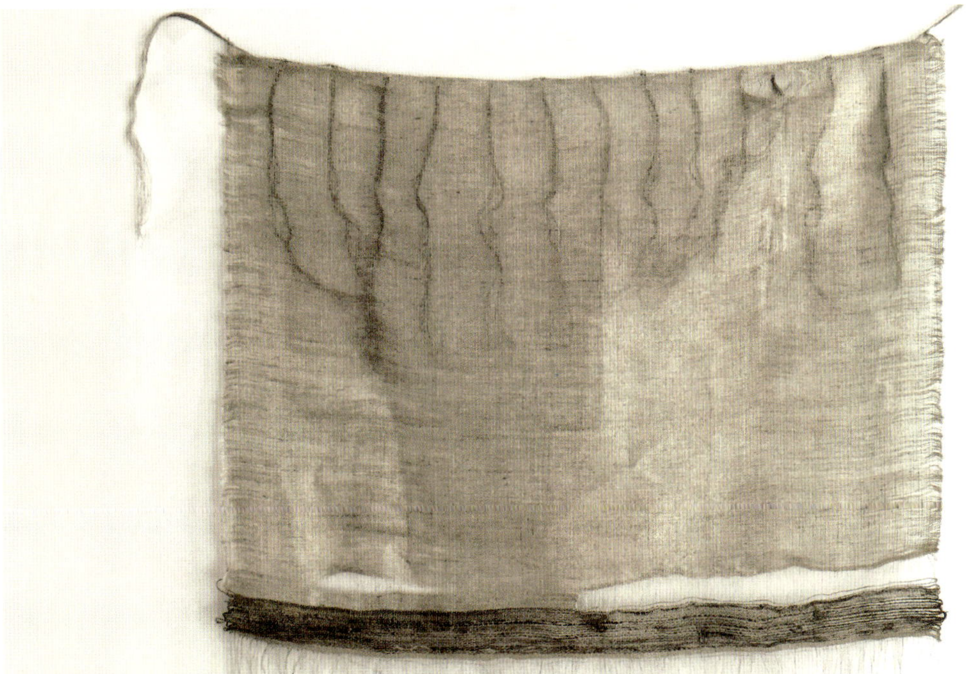

Weaving Art Pieces

Hand woven on a Japanese Saori loom, these pieces are slow-made with raw materials. The composition of each piece follows the material's properties such as the fiber's texture and color as well as the yarn's consistency.

Tools: Saori loom, Saori shuttle, yarn swift
Materials: Nettle, hemp, chunky forest silk, khadi cotton yarn, olive wood branch.

Weaving art pieces (details).

"Inside this world of alienation and through this vast network, I would like my work to carry the message that slow procedures, natural materials, an ethical approach and human expression still exist. The physical world still exists and it is full of life."

Morgan Hale | America

· Morgan Hale ·

Artist Morgan Hale's work aims to be ethereal and relaxing, evoking a feeling of calm in the viewer. Her pieces focus on melding the texture, pattern and color of mid-century and vintage designs with a modern, minimalist aesthetic. She loves the pastel color palettes of mid-century home design, specifically in kitchens and bathrooms. She has drawn much inspiration from pieces of home decor like jadeite glassware, milk glass, Pyrex patterns, atomic-style textiles, as well as from home interior elements like checkerboard floors, patterned Formica countertops with metal trim, light pink powder rooms, baby blue bathtubs and mint green sinks.

While she enjoys working in a variety of mediums, her main focus and love is weaving on her large floor loom. She finds the process of weaving relaxing and meditative, and is propelled by its repetitive rhythm and movement. Morgan has always been a tactile person with an interest in textiles, but her first introduction to weaving was during a college tour of the fibers department. During this tour, she saw the large wooden floor looms, overflowing yarn closet and inviting studio spaces. These alluring spaces drew her to learn more about weaving. Morgan graduated from Massachusetts College of Art and Design with a Bachelor of Fine Arts in fibers in 2014. She currently works from her home studio in New York City. For Morgan, keeping a cozy, curated and organized space has always been important to maintaining a productive and inspired workflow.

1. Please tell us your daily working schedule.

Planning is a big part of my life, so my day usually starts with a cup of tea and a list. This helps me get oriented and allows me to outline my day. My daily Moleskine planner along with quite a few Post-it notes helps me keep track of ongoing ideas, notes and reminders. I usually prefer to start my day with smaller tasks or administrative work and then I like to dive into weaving, warp winding, dyeing or other more hands-on tasks.

2. Where do you get inspiration for weaving?

Inspiration for my weavings comes from many different places. I spent most of my childhood in rural Vermont, so I have drawn much inspiration from the natural beauty of New England. I have lived in cities for the last few years and escaping to nature has always been a great reset for me. Fiber artists are also a huge inspiration. I love big coffee table books. I own *Beyond Craft: the Art of Fabric* and *Fiber: Sculpture 1960-Present* and reference these books often. They are both very inspiring and show a wide range of fiber art throughout time. I have also drawn inspiration from different branches of design—interior, graphic, furniture and architecture. I particularly love interior design and all the elements that come together to create it. Much of my recent work is inspired by mid-century home design and colors.

3. Please talk about the yarn you use. How do you find the most suitable yarn for your work?

In college, I started using linen for many of my less conventional pieces. I love the duality of linen—it has a rigid structure before washing, but after washing, it becomes wonderfully soft. As I became interested in working on utilitarian pieces, I started to try out other materials. I currently like to work with alpaca silk blend yarns, alpaca yarn, and cotton yarns. An alpaca silk blend is very soft and has a lovely drape to it. 100% alpaca is soft and has a nice drape as well, but it can be felted unlike a blend that contains silk. Pieces like scarves and cowls are great in alpaca and alpaca silk yarns. Cotton is a great everyday yarn and is perfect for items that are used more frequently, such as blankets and hand towels. Linen is also a great option for hand towels as it is very absorbent and will get softer with each use. I have tried out many different yarns to find my favorites. I'm a creature of habit and will generally stick to a material for quite some time.

4. You created experimental works before 2016. Now, your weaving is more relaxed. How did this change happen?

During and just after college, I had a lot of freedom to make less traditional work. Most of my pieces focused

on using weaving as the main structure and then had additional components. I collected and used buffalo teeth and various other animal bones as well as plaster in these pieces. Combining these harder materials with the softness of weaving was something that intrigued me. I also used these pieces to talk about and explore themes of time, recurrence, chance and memory. After school ended, I continued with this practice for some time but, eventually, I decided to shift my work towards more functional pieces. I had also worked as a production weaver for a baby wrap company during college, but creating functional work was something I hadn't experimented with on my own yet. I enjoyed making iterations and knew that I wanted to work on home goods and wearable products of my own.

5. Please tell us the story about your loom.

I have a Macomber Ad-a-Harness loom, which was gifted to me during college. My friend and studio mate worked at a museum. Her boss was an alum from our college and she wanted to find a good home for her old loom. My friend already had a loom of her own, so she let me know it was available and I jumped on the incredible opportunity.The loom even came with a bench, several tools and the original catalog from 1986, which is very fun to look at. For a long time, I kept a postcard taped to the front of my loom. The postcard shows one giant potato on a train car with a tiny man standing on top of the potato. I found it at a thrift store and loved how silly it was. These days, the postcard lives above my desk and not on the loom. My loom is also quite well-traveled. It has moved across the country with me twice—from Boston to San Francisco, then from San Francisco to New York City. It's still as sturdy as ever.

6. What other hobbies or passions do you have besides weaving?

Another creative passion of mine is photography. I photograph my work digitally and enjoy the process of composing a setting. It's also a great way to reflect on the work I've just finished and see the piece in its final form. Besides photographing my woven work, I like to shoot analog photos. I used to photograph with a Minolta film camera, but I now have a Polaroid instant camera that I use more. Aside from weaving and photography, I enjoy baking, taking care of my house plants, hanging out with my cat, going to live music events, traveling and trying out new restaurants and bars with friends.

˄ Burst Scarf

"Burst scarf" is a part of a collection of pieces inspired by mid-century shapes and colors. Morgan chose colors that contrast yet play nicely with each other. This deflected double weave pattern displays one of each color more prominently on each side and lets a little pop of the contrasting color come through.

Tools: Macomber floor loom, shuttles, bobbins, warp winder, bobbin winder, scissors, tape measure
Materials: alpaca silk

› Boxy Scarf

"Boxy scarf" is the most recent addition to her collection that was inspired by mid-century design. Morgan chose to use a deflected double weave pattern in a thick alpaca yarn and altered it to include three colors. After weaving and finishing, she wet felted each piece to soften the look and stabilize the floating yarns.

Tools: Macomber floor loom, shuttles, bobbins, warp winder, bobbin winder, scissors, tape measure, wet felting tools: hot water, soap
Materials: alpaca silk

˄ Color Block Mini Blanket

The color block mini blanket uses a diamond twill pattern to blend colors. By using three warp colors and the same three weft colors, overlapping blocks of color were created. Creating this blanket was a chance to mix colors in a painterly way to create a dynamic piece.

Tools: Macomber floor Loom, shuttles, bobbins, warp winder, bobbin winder, scissors, tape measure, sewing machine
Materials: Cotton

› Echo Blanket and Pillows

In these pieces, Morgan used a pattern called spider weave to provide dimension and visual complexity. To further emphasize this, she chose chunky yarns and made variations to the original pattern. These pattern and yarn choices help create a visual break from the grid structure that most weaving patterns follow.

Tools: Macomber floor loom, shuttles, bobbins, warp winder, bobbin winder, scissors, tape measure, sewing machine (for pillows)
Materials: cotton, New Zealand wool

FATSO

Tammy Kanat | Australia

· **Tammy Kanat** ·

Tammy Kanat was a jewelry designer. She launched Mink Jewelry, which quickly grew from a local, small scale, handmade business to an offshore, mass-produced operation. Mink became more about a business than about creativity. Wanting her art to be about the creativity, Tammy diverted her artistic talents to textiles. Her weaving journey began in 2011 when she enrolled in the highly-reputed Australian Tapestry Workshop to learn and refine the complex skill of tapestry weaving.

Tammy likes to explore and experiment with fiber to create an impact. She is curious to see what is possible. She likes the fact the people are drawn to the work and are curious enough to move toward it and touch it. She loves the way people see so many different things in her works from coral, sliced agate, desert rock to eyes and so on.

The color matching of Tammy's works is eye-catching. She is obsessed with color. It fascinates her how colors work together and the color combinations are endless. She likes to challenge everyone's relationship with color. She sees color as a story or a musical piece. The colors talk to each other and when they work, it is a beautiful experience.

Now, Tammy has gained international recognition through social media for her vibrant, uplifting work and has since produced commissioned works for local and international clients. She believes weaving is an ever-evolving and timeless art and an enchanting way to share the impact of her surroundings.

1. Please share with us your weaving process from conception to creation.

I usually start my work with a sense of excitement because it is not done and I don't know what it will look like. Only when the piece is complete will I truly know what it will look like. I find that once I get started, the work flows. I tend to start with a color. I choose something that resonates with how I am feeling that day and begin from there. My work is instinctive. There are not too many methods or systems involved. I generally find that once I'm in a piece, it's just like I have got to get to the end. I just want to know what happens, like getting to the end of a good book you are reading. Because I don't know, I don't plan. Planning makes me nervous.

2. How do you get inspiration and transform your thoughts into various patterns?

As an artist, I am inspired by many and varied things, from a floor tile to a landscape, from textile designers such as Gunta Stolzl to interior designers like Kelly Wearstler. There are so many incredible artists and creative people all around us. I am constantly inspired by interiors, buildings, fashion books, Instagram, podcasts and so on. My brain is always ticking and looking at my surroundings for a spark to work on a new creative idea. Creating is such a buzz and my most creative ideas often happen through mistakes. Then, I start to create something out of nothing.

3. Please tell us a bit about your chosen techniques and how you use them.

I use a mixture of techniques, some stem from traditional tapestry weaving and other techniques I have created while experimenting on my loom. I often find an exciting

new technique through mistakes. I thrive on imperfection. I believe it can make the work much more interesting and unique. The imperfections enable the light to shine through the cracks.

4. You've created many fantastic custom tapestries. How did you negotiate with your customer to ensure the outcome is satisfying for both you and your customer?

I believe when a customer gives me free rein to create a piece, they will get the best results. I always create unique works that connect with the brief I am given. I always give 100% to every piece and I believe mutual trust makes the outcome satisfying for the customer and me. Each piece I create is a part of me and I would prefer to keep my work if it is not connecting with someone. This is very important to me. The art does not stop with me. It continues in its new home.

5. What challenges did you meet in your career as a fabric artist?

It is challenging to make a living as an artist. However, I have been fortunate enough to establish a strong customer base. I have had a very positive response to my art form from the beginning and have continued to have commissions from around the globe. Something I am very proud of is that I am a self-taught artist and have created my unique style. My biggest challenge has been to not feel disappointed if I can't meet all the demands. I constantly remind myself to stay focused and keep challenging myself creatively. You do your best work when you're not trying to please others. You're probably your best self when you are creating without ego.

6. What advice would you give to an aspiring textile artist?

I believe the trick to living and working creatively is to do it for yourself. A few years ago, a friend told me a story of a singer who came onstage and performed for an adoring crowd despite being sick. At the end of this intimate performance, an audience member thanked the singer for making the effort. The singer replied, "I don't do it for you. I come out because it makes me feel better." I believe this is when an artist creates their best work. When you're not trying to please others. Keep working hard, being curious and doing what you love.

Wilderness

Woven tapestry framed in copper.

Materials: wool, linen, silk, mohair

Rina Matsumura | Canada

· Rina Matsumura ·

Rina Matsumura is a Japanese-Canadian tapestry weaver from Calgary, Alberta, Canada. She is a self-taught weaver whose style is modern, embracing clean lines, details, and negative space. Most of her works were completed with negative space. She was initially drawn to the idea of the space as a way to show what is there within each row of the woven weft. The warp of the weave is usually hidden behind fibers that are woven over top of it and she wanted to expose the hidden, to show that the part that we don't usually see can be beautiful and important too. Exposing the bare warp threads through the use of negative space is also a way of representing the parts of us that we don't expose to the world, the parts we don't readily show. Rina is also a registered nurse with more than 15 years of experience who works in the area of mental health. Weaving has given her comfort, a way to personally work through her anxiety and stress and has provided her with a quiet space to reset and rejuvenate. She wanted to merge her passions for weaving and mental health advocacy, to have them complemented and worked together as her art holds within the stories of her struggles and experiences as well as her experiences through helping others who are struggling. She wants to share with others what weaving has provided for her as well as gives back to the community. She's dedicated to helping through donations from pieces that she sells. Avelane Wall Art, her weaving brand, was formed as a way to showcase her woven wall hangings and represent her passion for creativity and mental health advocacy.

1. You call yourself a self-taught weaver. Could you please share with us your learning experience? What has been your greatest challenge while learning weaving?

Weaving, I believe, in some ways cannot be taught. It is an art form where you can learn some basic skills. However, I believe the expression of art comes from within. Since starting my weaving journey, I have been working to find my style and techniques. When trying new ideas, I often find myself in a cycle of trial and error, many times having to undo and redo work to get the aesthetic just the way I want. There have been times when I have to step away from a piece for a few days after struggling to work through an idea that isn't working, to clear my mind and then come back to it with less stress and fresh ideas. There is no greater feeling of pride and success than when I look at the finished piece and know that there was a journey and struggle to get there. Conversely, seeing weaving as an art form has brought its own set of challenges, the biggest is staying true to my style and avoid comparing it to what others are doing.

2. Please share with us your weaving process from conception to creation.

My creative process is one that is more freestyle. I tend to have an idea and just start weaving. I don't sketch out my pieces first as there is an internal urgency to get my ideas on the loom right away. I always start my pieces from the bottom, working upwards starting with the fringe. The fringe is worked on until it looks just right and this can mean taking it apart, mixing different fibers and cutting and trimming over and over until I am satisfied. I often spend a lot of time on the fringe before moving on to the body of the piece. The body of the piece is the transformation of my vision into fiber and again I work until I get the visual aesthetic just the way I want it to be. I have often reworked certain parts, changed color combinations and textures to get a piece to look the way I want it to. From conception to creation can be time-consuming. At times, pieces are being worked on and then left aside for some time. I have come to respect the artistic process and realize that sometimes I need to walk away and leave a piece to allow for the creative inspiration to return and give me the energy to complete it.

3. We noticed that your works combine various fibers. What types of fibers do you often use? Why?

Using different types of fiber, different in texture, composition and color, provides visual interest, personality and character to a finished piece. I often choose fibers based on the design ideas and flow of the

piece. I prefer linen blend fibers for my fringes. I find they have a silkier texture and hang beautifully. Most of my pieces that incorporate some color though my preference are usually neutrals and lighter weight fibers. I try to use fibers that are locally sourced and produced, and those come from animal or plant-based fibers. I am conscious of where my materials come from and how they are produced. It is important for me to uphold my personal beliefs about consumption and sustainability when choosing materials for my art pieces.

4. Please tell us a bit about your chosen techniques and how you use them.

The techniques I choose to use regularly in my work produce clean lines and details and allow the beauty of the simplicity to shine through. My techniques are flatter. I don't tend to use thick, roving-type fibers and choose to give texture to my pieces by using variances in my stitches. Varying my stitches provides visual interest. Using a simple over-under weave next to an abstract weave with no pattern can provide contrast and texture. The negative space technique is one that I enjoy, one that provides a challenge in each piece and a technique that provides additional texture and design detail. I try to use my favorite techniques to complement to each other in pieces, trying to push the design detail further with each new design. Pushing the limits of my artwork inspires me to keep trying new things.

5. How do you get inspiration and transform your thoughts into the various patterns?

I often have to think about how my thoughts will transform into a woven piece of art, how to design and work different aspects of my technique to bring my ideas into reality. I get inspiration from fibers that I see that have textures and colors that spark ideas. I also get inspiration from other art forms, a design I see painted on a ceramic mug, a painting I see in a museum or color combinations I see on a person's clothing. Finally, inspiration comes from the feelings and thoughts that I wish to convey through my art. My art is a vehicle for my own emotions and vulnerabilities to be displayed. I don't know how to describe how my ideas and thoughts get transformed into design other than to say that I tend to get an idea and get started. I often have multiple projects going at any given time as I start when inspiration comes to me rather than holding off.

6. What has been your greatest challenge to date? How did you conquer it?

I think the biggest challenge for me has always been perspective. Seeing my art for what it is, appreciating it for what it is and not allowing what was supposed to be a way to relieve stress and anxiety to become a source of it. I have to remind myself that what I am doing is not about producing and being the best. In a world where social media exposes us to a lot of great things, it can also be a source of comparison and pressure. I'm always reminding myself that my art can't be rushed, that my stories can't be rushed and that art and creativity can't be judged, and that this is the true beauty of art.

‹ Purple Patchwork Fish

"Purple Patchwork Fish" is a small woven wall hanging with a fiber-wrapped macramé cord fish, colorful patchwork, and negative space detail. The fish shape gives this piece a fun and whimsical feel and creates visual interest.

Tools: small frame loom, sewing needle and thread
Materials: various fibers, macramé cord, sewing thread, wooden dowel

˄ Mountain Trio

A special mountain landscape trio created to represent three siblings. The piece is showcased together as seen through the cohesive flowing fringe line, but can be separated into three separate pieces for each sibling to keep.

Tools: large frame loom
Materials: various fibers, embroidery thread, wooden dowel

˄ Framed Yellow Modern Abstract

"Framed Yellow Modern Abstract" is a modern weaving with a twist. The sharp yellow of this piece is contrasted by the black background acrylic paint on canvas. The dark background highlights the light warp threads in the negative space and brightens the colors of the patchwork detail. The final tapestry is mounted on canvas and framed for a modern finish.

Tools: medium frame loom, black acrylic paint, small paint roller, fabric glue for mounting, sewing needle, thread
Materials: various fibers, canvas, frame, macramé cord, sewing thread, wooden dowel

› Multicolor Window with Two-Tone Fringe

The multicolor negative space of the project is weaving with a wavy, double-layered fringe, open negative space and added yarn loop detail. The fiber-wrapped abstract shape provides the negative space while the multicolored yarn adds texture and dimension to the final piece.

Tools: medium frame loom, sewing needle and thread
Materials: various fibers, macramé cord, sewing thread, wooden dowel

IMAGINE

Allyson Rousseau | Canada

· **Allyson Rousseau** ·

Allyson Rousseau is a fiber artist and designer, born and based in Montréal, Quebec, Canada. With a degree in fine arts (2014) from the University of Guelph, Allyson has studied and worked with a wide range of media including woodworking and welding.

It wasn't until her final year of study that she began to teach herself how to weave, and newly discover and develop an interest in the juxtaposition of traditionally woven textiles and contemporary woven fiber art. Allyson has since turned her research and interest into a full-time, self-taught artistic practice. Her experiences with different media have contributed to her confidence in being able to control and manipulate materials. Her experience in woodworking was very valuable in learning about how to handle wood and tools of all kinds, which she uses every day for the looms that she makes as well as the dowels she uses to hang her work with once it's off the loom. Her background in painting and drawing has undoubtedly influenced her design aesthetic and artistic style as well. The most representative feature of her works is her choice of color. When choosing a color palette, Allyson is also paying equal attention to the type of the fiber and how it will react to being flat-woven or knotted as a raised element. She has created works for private collectors across the globe. The list of countries wherein her work resides includes Australia, South Korea, Turkey, Germany, Switzerland, Italy, France, Norway and the United States. Allyson has exhibited work in both solo and group exhibitions in Canada, the United States and Europe.

1. Please share with us your weaving process from conception to creation.

My weaving process varies depending on each piece that I make, but I will typically begin by choosing the color palette. I look through all of my materials and pick out one color of yarn that I would like to work with and then add to the palette with one more color at a time until I feel like it's balanced. I don't sketch out my ideas before weaving. I prefer to start by warping my loom for the size that I want the piece to be and then from there I choose my base color and begin weaving. If I have a design idea in mind, I'll work out the dimensions and measurements as I weave, making sure that it's well-balanced proportionately. If I want the piece to have raised areas in the design, I will weave all of the flat areas first and then fill in the open spaces with rya knots to create different levels in dimension and texture.

Sometimes, midway through the piece, I'll decide that I don't love one or more of the colors or types of fiber that I chose and I will remove them and re-work the palette until I'm happy with it. Only when I feel that weaving is well balanced in color, form and space will I cut it off of the loom. Once it's off the loom, I'll tie any loose ends on the back and attach a dowel to either just the top or both the top and bottom depending on the desired look.

2. The colors you use are fresh and pleasant. Do you have a method for choosing color palettes?

Out of habit lately, I work with a lot of blues, reds and yellows. There are so many tones and shades to explore within each hue of color that there is no limit to the possibilities. I always start by choosing one main color. This could either be the color of the base of the weaving or for a focal element. When I'm choosing colors, I'm also paying equal attention to the type of fiber and how it will react to being woven as the flat-woven base or the raised elements. I work with relatively small color palettes, typically choosing between three and five different colors or shades of a color. If I want the background of a piece to be white, I'll choose the material strictly for the type and texture of the yarn. The color palette is complete when I feel like it's well- rounded or balanced.

3. Please tell us a bit about your chosen techniques and how you use them.

I use a very simple and standard frame loom weaving technique. The two main weaving techniques that I use are plain weaving and rya knots. I plain weave all of my work, which is the classic over-under-over-under weave and I use rya knots to create both low- and high-pile areas.

Magnets.

There are a few other techniques that I have developed over the years in my work, which help to secure and finish the weaving, but due to having taught myself how to weave without any visual or written resources, I'm not sure if they have a specific name. If you're curious—you can watch and learn how I weave in my online classes.

4. The elements of your works are mostly graphic shapes. How do you get inspiration and transform your thoughts into the various patterns?

I am most inspired or influenced by my everyday surroundings. I often find myself conceptualizing an idea from details in the architecture of a building or something as mundane as painted lines on the street. Other times, I am inspired by how light affects our interpretation of color and I'll create a gradient from light to dark or dark to light, or both side by side—simply to study the differences in how my eyes see them at first glance.

Weaving with fibers as a medium to make art is very organic and fluid. I enjoy the process of using these soft materials to create a rigid design. This is also true and visible in the density that I weave. I weave with the intent of hiding any sign of warp in the design, which creates a really solid weaving with clean selvages (edges). The graphic shapes that I include in my designs work really well with this process and often end up looking more like a painting than a weaving from a distance. The fringe and the dowels on my work are present to remind the viewer of the medium.

5. We noticed that you also create custom pieces for clients. How do you negotiate with your clients when your thoughts are different?

I do. My process for custom pieces varies from client to client, but I will typically begin by asking for preliminary information such as budget, desired dimension and quantities, color or material preferences, timeline, etc. Sometimes clients will want me to re-create a piece either exactly like or close to one that I have made previously or they will give me full control over the design. In cases where clients aren't happy with the custom design or color palette, I will work with them by suggesting alternatives and we'll reach a point of compromise. If I strongly feel that the piece would look best a certain way, I will give my open and honest opinion (which is usually based on past experiences), and if the client still isn't happy with it, I will continue to work with them until they are satisfied. I enjoy the custom work process because it enables me to connect with people over my work on a more intimate level. It's much different than selling already-made work on my website because, for the most part, I may never have any contact with those customers. It can feel very surreal to send work out to people that I don't know, but it's also really incredible to know that I have work in the homes of hundreds of people in countries all around the world.

Number 9.

‹ Gradient Study

This was the first piece that Allyson made in 2018. It signified the beginning of her exploration of color blending and gradient studies. This piece was exhibited in a duo exhibition in Ottawa, Ontario, Canada in the winter of 2018.

Tools: handmade wooden frame loom, metal weaving needle, scissors small comb.
Materials: variety of natural, synthetic-blend fibers

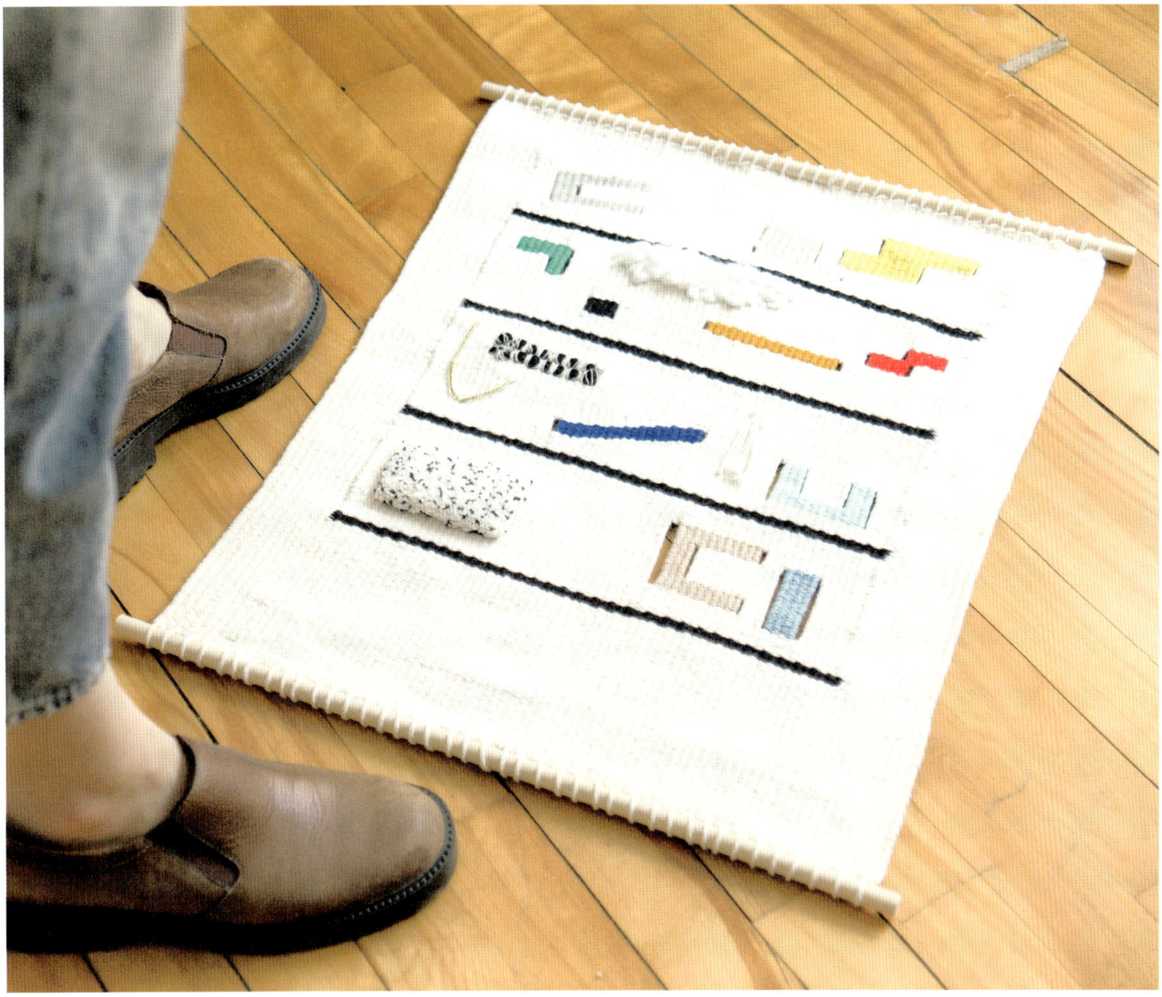

^ **Shapes on Shelves 2**

This piece was shown in the exhibition "Suspended Shapes" throughout the summer of 2017 in Lansing, Michigan.

Materials: A variety of natural and synthetic fibers, wooden dowels

The Ninevites | South Africa

· The Ninevites ·

The Ninevites is a design studio and collaborative platform founded by Nkuli Mlangeni-Berg. The Ninevites makes beautiful things, inventive designs with made-to-be-touched textures. It makes gorgeous objects that take pride of place in discerning homes. However, The Ninevites is more than that. It is telling a story, too. It is a story about culture and unheard voices, age-old traditions in a modern context, heritage and handicraft. It gathers threads from across the continent and weaves them all into a beautiful story. The textiles The Ninevites uses are meticulously handcrafted by artisans in the Cape Town, South Africa and Lima, Peru using 100% South African-grown mohair and Peruvian sheep wool. The mohair is sourced from Eastern Cape farms that are monitored by the organization South African Mohair. It is both durable and resilient, and notable for its high luster, sheen soft and luxurious fiber. It feels plush and soft underfoot. Mohair is the fleece of the Angora goat and it is one of the world's most beautiful sustainable natural fibers. It is warm in winter and has excellent insulating properties while remaining cool in summer due to its moisture absorbing properties. Empowered by their handicrafts, the artisans in The Ninevites hand spin and dye the raw fiber using trusted techniques to ensure exceptional quality and durability. The bold, geometric patterns of The Ninevites' works are inspired by traditional patterns in African basketry, pottery, murals and beading to express the untold stories of indigenous Southern African craft in vivid, visceral form.

1. You said that you are telling a story. What story do you want to tell?

I wanted to tell a story of my people. For many years, the story of black people and Africa was told by others and often it was told to suit the other. I wanted to use our arts to tell the story about our culture in a way that I saw it when I grew up, so that my daughter and future generations know where we come from as a people.

2. The weaving materials of your products are South African-grown mohair and Peruvian sheep's wool. Could you please share with us some of your knowledge of mohair and Peruvian sheep's wool?

South Africa and Lesotho produce a lot of mohair but, unfortunately, it is often auctioned to China and then sold back to us. It's a very beautiful luxurious fiber and could be contributing to the economy of our country, but it's not. The texture of mohair is very beautiful and long-lasting. And the Peruvian wool is the finest thing to weave. Peruvian wool is light and very fine whereas mohair is thick and heavy.

3. You dye the textiles yourself. Do you use natural dyes to create colors? What's the most important step during the dyeing process?

All the textiles are hand dyed. For the Peruvian yarn we only use natural dyes sourced from the area and for the South African mohair, we use chemical dyes due to lack of access to the materials. The region where we weave does not have much water. It's a desert and difficult to grow natural dyes.

Since there is no machine, the process is very organic and the outcome is not always exact. One rug is not the same as the next one because it may be woven by a different weaver, and their hands and ways of weaving are different.

4. With the development of machinery, more and more traditional crafts are gradually disappearing. Why do you want to revive traditional weaving and make it a new industry?

It is because the handmade traditional crafts are much more sustainable than machine production. You don't need any electricity to weave and using natural resources is less toxic for our planet. And we can learn a lot from ancient traditions and share our stories with the next generations.

5. The style of traditional crafts is not widely accepted in modern times. What would you do to meet this challenge? Have you created some innovations for your products?

I think that it's slowly changing. More and more people are starting to recognize crafts as an important medium in our society. And I like to keep things as organic as possible. I innovate in the designs, but the actual techniques are still old and still the ones used in the old days.

6. What are your hopes and future plans for the field of weaving?

My wish is to see that artisans are treated fairly so they can sustain themselves with a craft and that people see the importance of slowing down a little, producing less and not consuming much. I also hope to use weaving as a form of healing our communities, and creating spaces and platforms where we can engage in conversations that affect as human, women and people.

Rug Collection

The unique collection is meticulously handcrafted by female artisans in the Western Cape using 100% South African-grown mohair. Empowered by their handicraft, these local women hand spin and dye the raw fiber using trusted techniques to ensure exceptional quality and durability. The bold, geometric patterns on these blankets and rugs are inspired by traditional basketry, pottery, murals and beading to express the untold stories of black South Africans in vivid, visceral form.

Materials: mohair, sheep wool

Every year, I spend a couple of weeks studying at the Kawashima textile school. It is a wonderful environment where I can weave, learn and explore different techniques. Spending the time there and boarding at the school allows me to focus on just the weaving without any distractions that arise from normal daily life at home.

4. Please share with us your weaving process from conception to creation.

When I create a weaving, I always start with a hand-drawn sketch. I then will hand dye all my Australian wool naturally and with Australian wool dyes when they are still in skeins. They then will be winded and ready to weave. After I warp my loom, I create my weavings only using my hands as tools, nothing else.

5. The work "Weaving Scarlett" is very expressive. How long did it take to weave the portrait? What was the most difficult step during the process?

"Weaving Scarlett" is a significant piece to me. It is my daughter as a baby. Her piercing blue eyes are reflected in the piece and I feel when you look at the weaving it is like she is looking into your soul. The piece took me over three months, weaving full-time and it was difficult to achieve the eyes, mouth and nose. I am very happy the way she turned out and she now hangs in my daughter's bedroom.

6. You also give lessons. What does it mean to you?

I have been teaching tapestry weaving for seven years all around the world. I love teaching the ancient craft in a contemporary manner. My students love all my colors and textures that I offer in a class. I love how each student work is so unique and how they place the wools to create their masterpieces.

‹ Woven Dreams Series

The "Woven Dreams Series" was woven with hand-dyed wool.

Materials: hand-dyed wool

PHOTOGRAPHY: **Ashley Mackevicius (photo on page 120).**

› Weaving Scarlett

"Weaving Scarlett" is the weaving portrait of Natalie's daughter.

Materials: hand-dyed wool

"Her piercing blue eyes are reflected in the piece and I feel when you look at the weaving it is like she is looking into your soul."

Evee Erb | America

· **Evee Erb** ·

Evee Erb is an interdisciplinary artist who received her bachelor of fine arts degree from the Maryland Institute College of Art (MICA) in 2016. While attending MICA, she also studied illustration and textile design. Additionally, Evee studied in Florence, Italy at SACI College of Art and Design. After completing her degree, Evee returned to her hometown of Durham, North Carolina where she worked at the North Carolina Museum of Art, taught workshops at a variety of art centers, served on curatorial jury panels, and gave lessons and artist talks at various institutions. She also created her clothing label, Threadbarren, which is comprised of her hand-woven garments made by using naturally-dyed and recycled fibers. As a ceramic artist, Evee loves to experiment with different ways of combining ceramic and fiber. In her interdisciplinary studio practice, she works predominantly with fiber, ceramic and paint. She said, "Sculpture teaches me about weaving, weaving teaches me about painting and painting teaches me about sculpture." Woven textiles lend themselves to sculpture due to the strength and flexibility of its structure. Weaving is corporeal by nature—like the body, it is a spiritual container made of many interconnected parts. In this way, weaving is inherently related to figure sculpture. Weavings are vessels. Vertical warp threads bend and adapt to contain horizontal weft threads, forming strength in an interwoven cloth. Through the investigation of material, pattern and structure, Evee's work examines the relationship between gender, society and the individual. The figurative nature of weaving is revealed in its symmetry to the body as a vessel.

1. Please share with us your weaving process from conception to creation.

I begin by designing what is called a draft, which is a chart pattern dictating how threads are mounted onto the loom. By lifting the vertical warp threads on the loom in different successive pattern repeats, I can achieve different weave structures. After determining a color palette for the fiber, most weavers would then measure their yarn to ensure a proper gauge (called "sett") of the weave structure. However, I prefer not to calculate my sett and instead I employ a more intuitive selection process with my materials. Sometimes I weave samples to test a design and sometimes I just go straight ahead and see where the weaving process takes me. I only use my handspun yarn and recycled fibers in my work and have found more joy in taking an organic and experimental approach. To me, play and aesthetic instinct are the most important ingredients to any design.

2. Please tell us a bit about your chosen techniques and how you use them.

I love experimenting with texture in my weaving. One way I do this is by incorporating unconventional, raw materials into my work. For example, I recently finished a piece that was woven with pine needles embedded into the fiber. I am also a fringe-fanatic and love to add supplementary fringe to my pieces to achieve different compositions. I divide texture into two categories: tactile and visual. While a weaving may feel textured to the hand, it can still look flat from a distance. The combination of tactile and visual texture allows my weavings to be more dynamic from any vantage point. Visual texture is largely determined by the fiber content of a textile as well as its weave structure. One of my favorite structures is called overshot, which uses long weft floats supported by a traditional plain weave structure to create a stable yet highly patterned textile.

3. What types of textiles do you often use? Why? Will different materials affect the outcome of your works?

In my weaving practice, I strictly use only naturally dyed and recycled fibers. I live and work in North Carolina, which was once considered the textile capital of America. As production gradually shifted overseas in the 20th century, hundreds of textile mills were closed across the state. There is now an enormous amount of fiber mill waste needing to be recycled and reprocessed in my region. My use of recycled fibers is an attempt to aid in this endeavor, as well as raise awareness of unsustainable textile production. Different types of fiber have different properties and can, therefore, be used to produce different types of textiles. For example, protein fibers such as wool, cashmere, alpaca and mohair can be wet felted after weaving to create alofty, dense fabric. The locally sourced,

recycled fibers that I use are both natural and synthetic, and can lead to different results in the weaving process.

4. You also make ceramic sculptures. Do clay and weaving have something in common?

Absolutely! I refer to myself as an interdisciplinary artist, working and learning from a variety of media. There are many correlations between weaving and ceramics, which I am constantly discovering in my studio. Both involve traditionally utilitarian materials used to create functional objects such as cloth, basketry and pottery. From these objects, we can see perhaps the most important relationship between weaving and ceramics. In their essence, both are vessels. All types of weaving are formed in a three-dimensional structure of vertical warp threads, which contain horizontal weft threads. Woven structures are, in and of themselves, containers and may be further used as vessels in applications such as basketry. Meanwhile, all forms of ceramic sculptures and pottery must be hollow to be successfully fired in a kiln. In this way, weaving and ceramic sculpture are both physical vessels. In my work, I also see them as containers of spirit and artistic expression.

5. Your work is such a unique form of creativity. What do you want to express through your fiber works?

My artistic methodology is largely driven by the feminist movement. In a patriarchal Western art world, fiber art has historically been dismissed as "women's work"—the very meaning of which suggests that fiber art is a lesser art form because it is practiced by women. Remaining largely stigmatized to this day, fiber art is seen in many spheres as "low" or "folk art." For me, being a professional fiber artist is, in many ways, an act of rebellion. Through my work, I wish to celebrate women by championing fiber art as an equally valid art form as painting and sculpture. I see fiber art as reclamation of women's rights and a proclamation of equality. By expressing this in my work, I hope that it may empower others and change the perception of fiber art.

6. What has been your greatest challenge to date? How did you conquer it?

As a weaver, organization has been a challenge in several aspects. It can be difficult to stay tidy when you have a studio full of yarn. I have discovered that if I maintain an organized studio space, my thought process while working becomes clearer. This clarity is then reflected in my finished weavings. However, I believe my greatest challenge as an artist has been learning how to create continuity between materials. Weaving, ceramics and painting are all such technical art forms. When I began my interdisciplinary practice, it was difficult to imagine how such disparate materials and techniques could be used together harmoniously. Through years of study, testing and experimentation, I was able to create a more cohesive visual language by simultaneously working with multiple mediums. Developing this process has allowed me to become more versatile, while maintaining a clear direction in my work.

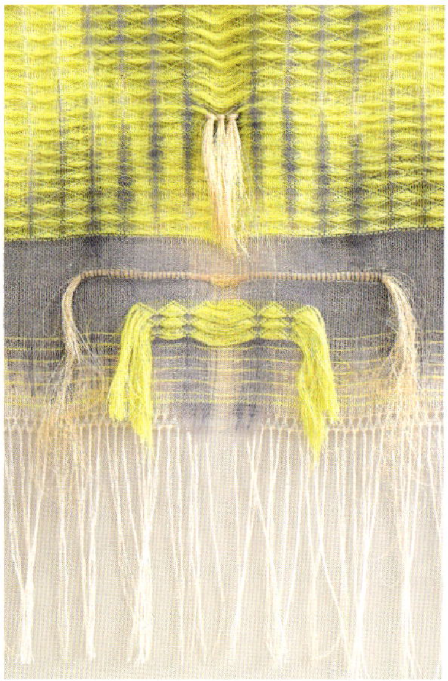

Detail.

Shroud of Hysteria (Escaping the Garden)

"Shroud of Hysteria" is a large weaving hanging from curtain rod. By sewing two panels together, Evee created this large-scale textile with silk that she naturally dyed using goldenrod and hibiscus flowers.

Tools: eight-shaft loom, spinning wheel, stainless steel dye pot
Materials: naturally-dyed silk, hand-spun and recycled fibers

Presence in Absence

In her use of paint on hand-woven textiles, Evee explores the push and pull of positive and negative space within her compositions.

Tools: eight-shaft loom, spinning wheel, sable paint brushes
Materials: oil on hand-woven textile, hand-spun, naturally dyed and recycled fibers

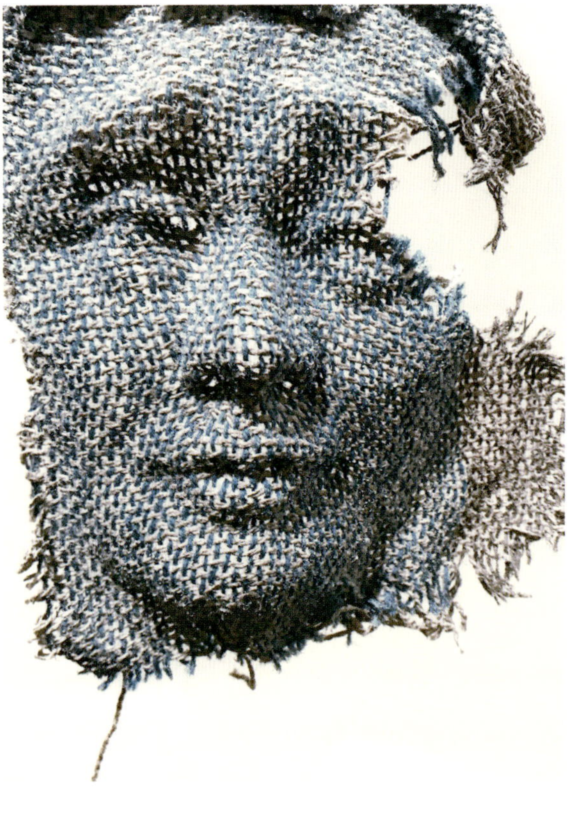

^ Solitude

A double weave structure is visible through the oil paint, adding a dimensional quality to the portrait.

Tools: eight-shaft loom, sable paint brushes
Materials: oil on hand-woven textile, hand-dyed and recycled fibers

Hannah Waldron | The United Kingdom

· **Hannah Waldron** ·

Hannah Waldron is an artist and designer based in the United Kingdom. Her graphic- and narrative-led image-making has been applied across a range of media from print to textiles at both a personal and architectural scale. In 2010, she spent six months in Berlin where she discovered the woven works of Anni Albers and Gunta Stolzl at the Bauhaus Archive and fell in love with their works. Hannah then bought a small loom and began experimenting and immediately could see lots of potential for exploring ideas in that weaving and, more broadly, textiles. She has found weaving to be a natural process to complement her grid-based image-making and, in 2014, she completed a master of fine arts degree in textiles at Konstfack, Sweden. Hannah specializes in designing and creating research-led unique printed and woven textiles that have an emphasis on storytelling. She has felt like weaving has brought out of her a desire to tell stories, the linear, rhythmic nature of the process is much like the structure of a story. She thinks there is a defined, beginning, middle and end to a weaving. There is such a rich history of tapestry being used as a vehicle for narrative and so much potential for updating the method to the contemporary visual landscape. From her point of view, it is because weaving is about applying a strict structure on materials, matter, which is like a story in itself. Her weaving is a way to craft unruly threads into an ordered, thought-about structure, which is very much like what a storyteller does.

1. Please share with us your weaving process from conception to creation.

The weavings I make are usually about a specific place, activity or a journey. I spend a lot of time making sketches and paintings of the different scenes, so to speak, and mapping which parts of the city or journey were essential to that story. In the same way, with each part of the narrative I try to reduce the information down again to the most essential, and then piece together these sections in a way that makes sense to me and also will work well on the loom, in the woven language. Then I make a life-size cartoon on graph paper, which I can put behind the warp to follow when I weave. I am very much interested in the tapestry tradition and how, in many cultures and throughout time, tapestry and textiles, in general, have been used as a way of communicating stories. So, this storytelling aspect is in the forefront of my mind and, although I am using my own experiences as the narrative, I don't particularly think it is my story that I am interested in telling. Instead, I'm exploring ways of storytelling that are becoming redundant in our society and are vitally important to protect.

2. The color matching of your works is eye-catching. Do you have a method for choosing color palettes?

I am fascinated by the impact of color and how colors can work powerfully together, for instance by studying color theory from Josef Albers' book *Interaction of Color*. I use color to evoke the experience of the subject matter, rather than directly replicate it. So, I will choose colors that I think conjure up an atmosphere of the narrative I want to tell and do this through selecting yarns together or making color palettes with gouache sketches.

3. How do you get inspiration and transform your thoughts into the various patterns?

When I began to weave, I found that the subjects I was choosing for the designs were cities and journeys. I find there is something in weaving that relates very well to mapping places and time. I think it is this grid of the loom. I see it almost like the axis of time and space in the warp and weft. Each weaving I make is a very subjective map of my experience of that place and I am exploring it in terms of color, form, texture and pattern.

I like best when you have the same texture or pattern, but repeating with slight variations, to explore one structure or texture in all its complexity you realize just how many possibilities there are in the world. It makes me think about the infinite nature of things in a way that's not too overwhelming.

4. Your work is such a unique form of creativity. What or who were the early influences on your style?

Thank you, that is a kind compliment to make. In terms of my visual language, I think the main influence was the weavers of the Bauhaus. They embraced the limitations of the loom, which often compels a distilled, abstracted language. It was the perfect moment as modernism embraced the essence of form and the structure of the grid at that time. It resulted in the invigoration of the medium of weaving and helped people to see the process with fresh eyes. It certainly did for me when I first saw them in Berlin and I try to embrace that approach to weaving—using the language of weaving with subject matter updated to the world we live in today.

5. What's the most important step during the creation of woven textiles?

That's a difficult question because every stage of the process seems intrinsically important. On a practical level, setting up the loom and getting the tension right is very important because it causes many issues if you don't get an even tension in the very beginning. But, perhaps it is most important to love the process, have a respect for the materials and take care at every step because it is very slow and time-consuming, so you have to be deeply invested, otherwise, it is a waste in many ways.

6. You also teach. Is that an interesting experience? What does it mean to you?

Yes, I have taught on many different occasions. I have run a week-long course at Saterglantan in Sweden for the past two years, and, most recently, I ran a workshop in Tokyo, Japan. I also regularly teach workshops and give lectures in the UK. Now that I have been a practitioner for 10 years, I feel glad and a sense of duty to share the knowledge I have built up (and that others, in turn, have taught me). It is also inspiring to see when people first come into contact with the process of weaving. It is like they discover a new language and I get quite a lot of energy from their enthusiasm. It reminds me of the scope of possibilities within the weaving.

^ Cloud in Hand

"Cloud in Hand," an intricate weaving based on the album *The Coral Sea* by Patti Smith, is a tapestry for the present. It celebrates Smith's luminous crafting of words to convey the physical world, as well as the inner world and hopes to translate the tactile qualities of *The Coral Sea* into the tactile, communicative language of weaving.

Tools: rigid heddle loom
Materials: wool, cotton, silk, indigo hand-dyed silk

‹ Map Tapestries

“Map Tapestries” is a series of tapestries that explores and documents experiences of time and place. Hannah maps the places she has visited, such as New York, Venice and Berlin as well as Minakami, a little village in Japan. In today’s world, where traveling fast is possible and we can view the world easily through satellite images, Hannah carefully examines and applies aspects of human interpretations on a landscape. The hangings, Map Tapestries, became personal monuments to her experiences, but also a relevant vehicle for exploring the world around us.

Tools: rigid heddle loom
Materials: cotton, wool, linen, silk, Tencel, bamboo

˄ Spans Series

The forms contained in this series link archetypal textile design language with the built environment. The compression and extension in the compositions continues Hannah’s interest in high speed travel, rhythm and acceleration in relation to the process of hand weaving.

Materials: wool, silk, cotton, linen, indigo, wood, SISTERS-WEAVING-HIRES madder

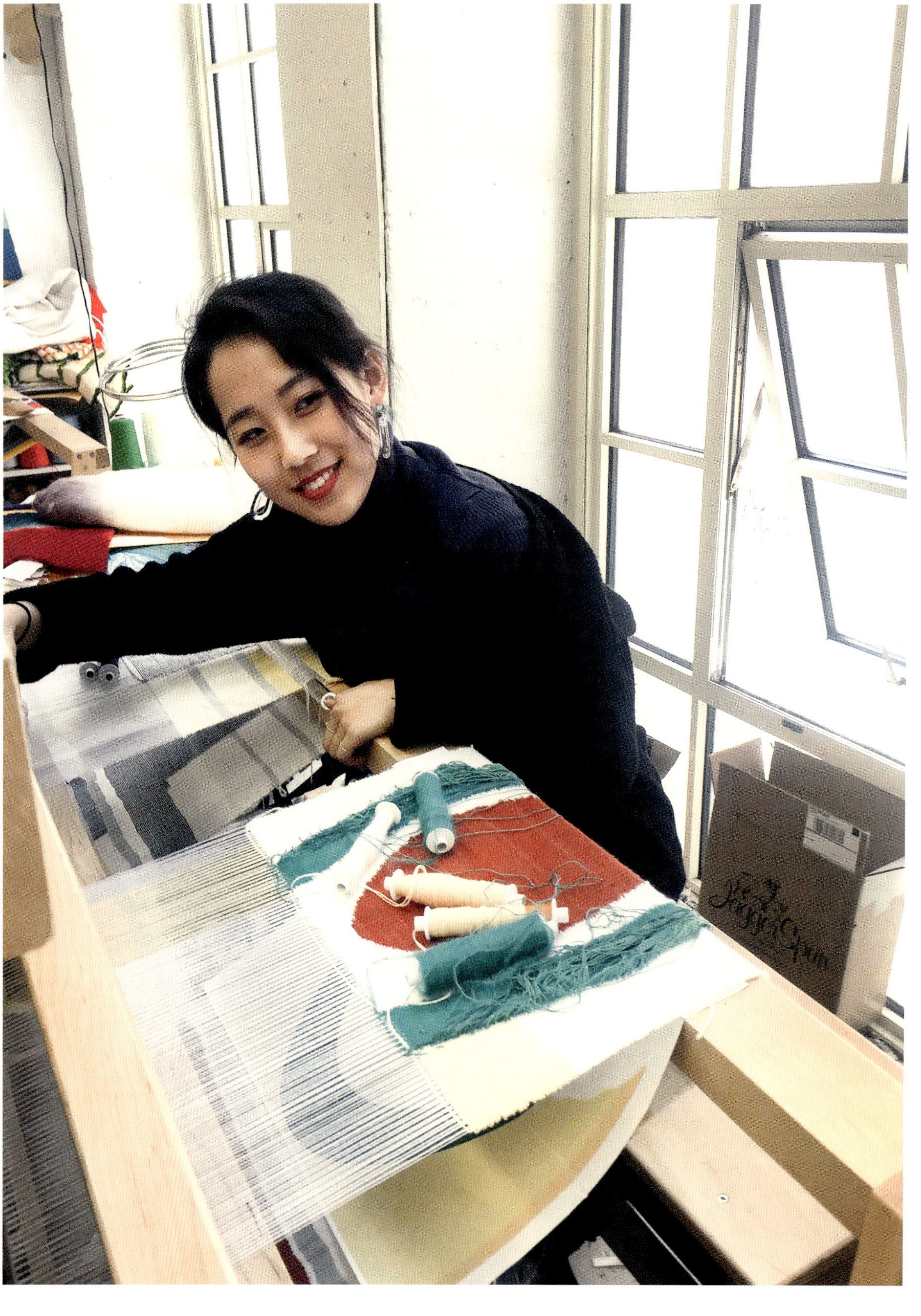
JaggerSpun

Kate Park | South Korea

· **Kate Park** ·

Kate Park is a textile artist and designer. She was born and raised in South Korea and is currently based in New York. She received her bachelor of fine arts degree in textiles from the Rhode Island School of Design. In her first year of school, she learned about textiles and the fact that one of the very first forms of computing and programming was a loom—a weaving machine. She had an epiphany that weaving is the perfect merge of art and engineering that she always had been searching for. Kate is interested in translating abstract ideas into visual reality using fiber manipulation and weaving. The major idea of the artist's work is a coexisting relationship between dual identities. As a Korean living in the United States, Kate suffered a constant identity crisis. The cultural adaptation resulted in her confused identity. But Kate slowly concluded that, although much of it felt like a struggle, it was also a great blessing to have a multi cultural upbringing. Kate later depicted such a positive approach in her works. Her series of textile works represent various explorations of the idea in hand or industrially woven panels engineered to stand as poetic structures. The artist's structural and three-dimensional textile work challenges the general and traditional conception of textiles.

1. Please share with us your weaving process from conception to creation.

I start with organizing my floating ideas and inspirations by writing and sketching. When the general direction is set, I begin collecting various materials to visually grasp the concept that I want to portray. Since I work better three-dimensionally, I move onto making small mock-ups. Sometimes I will get inspired by the happy accidents or realize the limitation of the technique through unexpected results. Once I have figured out the details such as size, form, structure, color and techniques I want to use, I start on my technical planning. This varies depending on what machine I decide to use. If using an industrial Jacquard, I begin to translate my drawings or paintings to a computerized format and if using a floor loom, I have to consider the type of fiber, density and weaving structure to set up the warp. Then I start the execution process. I weave, knit or felt to make the piece, often going through technical difficulties and problem-solving during the making phase. My final task is to work out the ideal way to install and present my artwork.

2. You sometimes dye fabrics yourself. Could you please share some knowledge about acid dye? Why do you choose to dye fabrics yourself?

I enjoy using acid dye. It is comparatively easy and fibers take in the dyes quickly and nicely. I like dyeing the fibers, yarn and fabric myself because I can not only have full control over hues, saturation and shade, but also manually manipulate how the dyes are taken in. For instance, I can use various dyeing techniques such as clamp dyeing, tie-dyeing and dip dyeing to achieve certain dye effects. Sometimes various fibers react differently in the same dye pot, which often ends up being a pleasant surprise.

3. We noticed that you use multiple fibers in your fiber works. Will different fibers achieve different visual effects? Could you please share some details with us?

I often mix multiple fibers in my textile pieces. I engineer the different fibers in my weavings sometimes to achieve subtle variation in surface or texture and sometimes to exaggerate certain fiber's natural tendency. For instance, I wove "Faithful, Constant, Always" using wool, mohair, cotton and polyester to achieve some subtle variations. I used mohair to be fluffy after brushed, polyester to add some shine, cotton to sit rather linear when hung and wool to hold all the fibers tightly. On the other hand, I engineered "Power of Limit" to maximize the contrast between wool and non-wool fibers when washed. The extra-fine merino wools felted and shrunk causing the

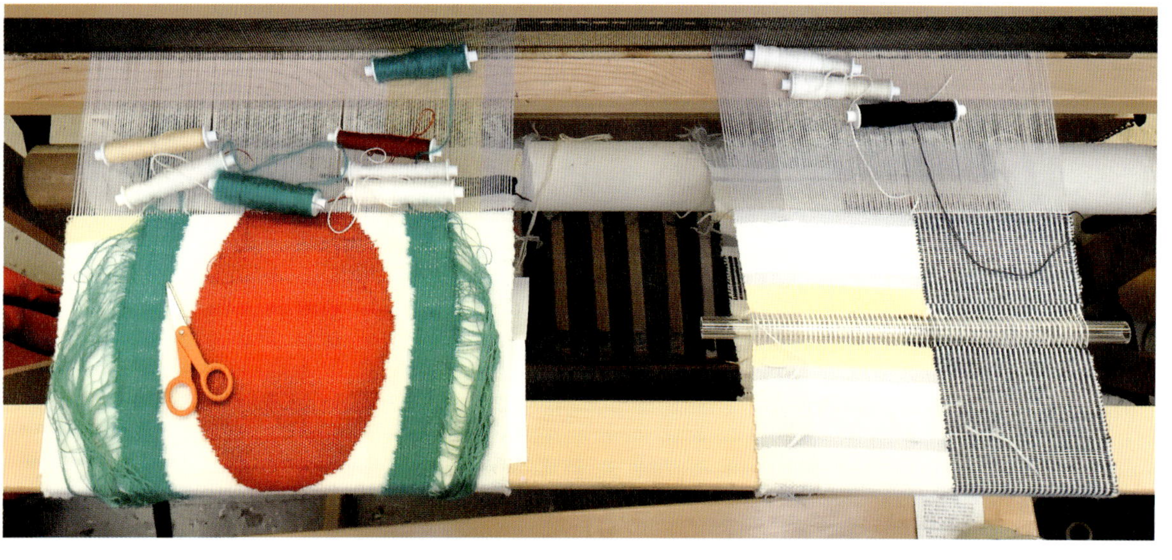

rayon and cotton surface to "ripple" in increasing and decreasing manners. Weaving with different fibers can not only achieve two-dimensional textural variation, but also accomplish three-dimensional structural variation.

4. Your three-dimensional textile works are unique. How do you get inspiration and transform your idea into visual reality?

Since I am working with quite abstract ideas, translating the idea into a visual textile piece is challenging. Consequently, writing and drawing are absolutely essential in my creative process. In order to find an original source of inspiration, I rely heavily on my own photography or even my memories. Although it is challenging to deal with abstract, but realistic ideas such as existence and relationships, I believe it allows me to create unique and poetic three-dimensional textile work.

5. You said that the major idea of your works is a coexisting relationship between dual identities. Could you tell us a bit more about it? Could you give us some examples?

The major idea throughout my body of work is indeed the coexisting relationship between dual identities. My earlier work deals with my cultural confusion caused by my dual identity as a Korean living in the United States. Later, I see my cultural dual identity in a brighter light and my positive approach is depicted in my work, including the piece "Coexistence"—a vibrant double-layered Jacquard reflecting the coexistence of past and present in Seoul and also mirroring the coexistence of my dual identity. In my more recent work, the focus has shifted to finding my new identity in faith and my inseparable coexistence with the higher being, God. This idea is depicted in the series "Faithful, Constant, Always," "Like the Moon Pulls the Tide," "Lost and Being Found" and "Power of Limit." Each piece has dual panels engineered to stand as poetic structures.

6. What's your hope and future plan for the field of weaving?

When I first started, I simply imagined myself making cute rugs for my home or pretty dresses. As much as I love making rugs and dresses, I also have observed and experienced the limitless possibility of textile art, design and technology. I am eager to explore the unknown of weaving, beyond art and design and even in technical textile in the fields of information technology or medicine. Weaving or fiber art is still a foreign field for many people. When people hear the word weaving, they just imagine someone in ancient days sitting and simply making clothes. I would love the general public to know that is just a mere glimpse into weaving and the present and future hold so much more potential in weaving. In addition to my job as a textile artist and designer, I see myself as a textile ambassador.

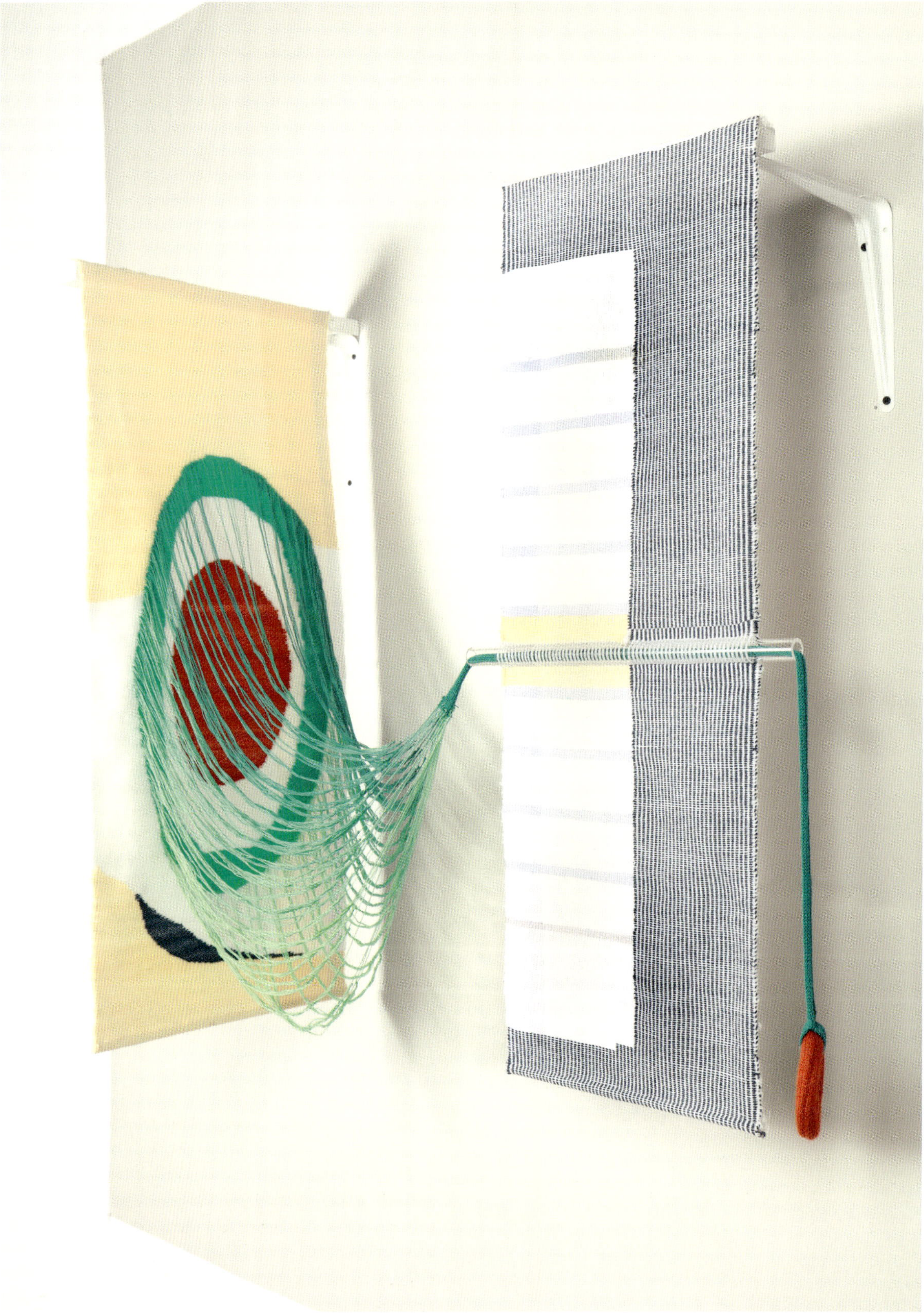

‹ Like the Moon Pulls the Tide

Like the moon pulls the tide. In oceans deep my faith will stand.

Tools: eight-harness floor loom
Materials: wool, mohair, cotton

ˆ Lost and Being Found

Constantly lost and being found for I am weak and he is strong.

Tools: eight-harness floor loom
Materials: wool, mohair, cotton, felt

^ Faithful, Constant, Always

You are faithful, constant and always. You are a stillness that moves.

Tools: eight-harness floor loom
Materials: wool, mohair, cotton, polyester

› Power of Limit

All patterns are defined by their limits and these limits give form to the limitless. This is the power of limit.
—György Dócz

Tools: Jacquard loom
Materials: wool, rayon, cotton

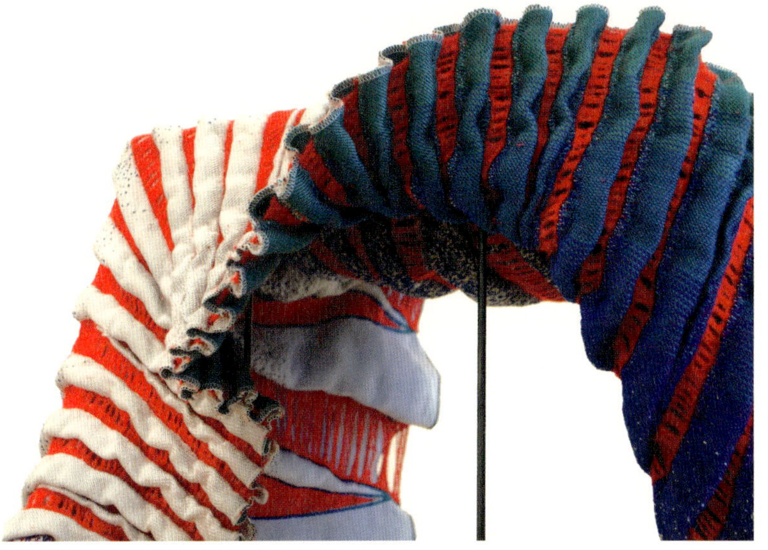

Tintsaba | Swaziland

· **Tintsaba** ·

Tintsaba was founded by Sheila Freemantle in 1985. Her focus was on how she could help the women of rural Swaziland take charge of their lives and become independent. Starting with only 12 local women, Sheila's guidance, dedication and innovation brought Tintsaba to what it is today. These qualities helped Tintsaba become renowned for refined, high-quality sisal basketry weaving, and recognized as an industry leader and awarded repeatedly over the years.

Since its inception, Tintsaba has endeavored to create a workplace that helps the women of rural Swaziland grow and develop themselves. Through various courses and workshops ranging in a variety of subjects such as leadership, skill-set development, training, environmental awareness, and women's health, the women of rural Swaziland pride themselves on encouraging a holistic approach not only in their works, but also in their daily lives.

Unfortunately, the founder Sheila Freemantle passed away in 2012. But with the dedication of her husband, Richard, the Tintsaba team continues in her memory. The team strives to uphold Sheila's ideals of excellence, teamwork, commitment to the earth and the holistic well-being of their groups.

During the last 30 years, Tintsaba has trained and worked with more than 1,000 women in rural Swaziland. Invoking Sheila's passion, the team is dedicated to creating the highest quality hand-woven sisal products. The future for Tintsaba and Swazi women is one of independence, the strength of self and to lead by example within communities.

1. Please share with us your weaving process from conception to creation.

The sisal fiber is separated from the succulent agave leaf using a straight blunt edge like a spade or the edge of a tin. The cleaned fiber is laid out and dried in the sunshine for a few days. It is then delivered to our workshop. Once checked, it is sent to be dyed in the wood-fired vats. After dyeing, it is hung to dry.

Our designer or customer (depending on the situation) will draw out or choose a design. This drawing or picture and the corresponding dyed sisal colors are then given to an artist. She will try to replicate it, but as each weaver is an artist herself, it will be an interpretation of what she sees.

The weaver then starts by spinning the fibers to make one continuous thread in each color, enough to complete the basket's design. Starting with creating the center coil, these threads are woven around a small amount of grass (coil core) in a growing spiral. The more skilled artists then create intricate patterns by alternating the different colors that show on the coils and thus creating the pattern and the final basket.

2. Tintsaba's products are made of sisal fiber. Could you please share with us some of your knowledge of sisal? Why do you choose sisal fibers to weave?

Sisal is sourced from the agave sisalana plant. Originally from Central America, sisal has been used all over the world for making string, rope and cordage. It is unknown when the plant made it to Africa. Tintsaba found the basket makers had been using sisal for many generations for their products. It grows wild and is, in fact, an invasive weed, so culling the noxious weed helps keep the local biodiversity intact. We only use the young leaves as the fiber, which is very white and can take the color dye well.

3. Could you please share with us the major steps of dyeing? What's the most important step during the process?

The dye processing requires clean water, accurate measures of dye pigment (we keep strict recipes down to the 0.1 of a gram) and a constant temperature that is close to boiling. It is important to have the sisal as clean as possible and we only use young sisal (this has the whitest

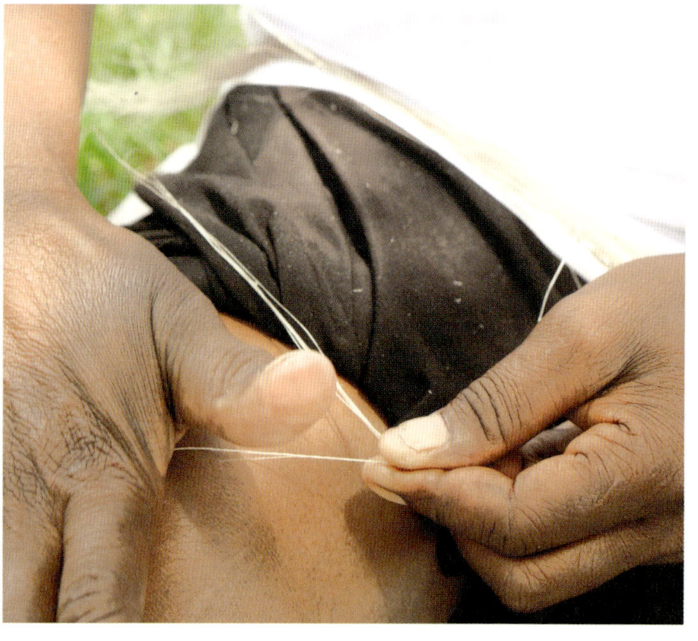

color), which helps bring out the vibrancy of the dye. The dye is added to the boiling water and stirred in. A small sample of sisal is added to check whether the color is correct and then all the sisal is added. The vats are left to boil for 20–45 minutes, depending on the color needed and the recipe. Once the time is up, the sisal is put in a cooling bath to stop the dyeing process and cool down the fiber. It is also cleaned and checked. When ready, the now-dyed sisal is hung to dry for a few days. When it's dry, it is ready to go to a weaver.

4. The products you have created are exquisite with a unique style. How do you get inspiration?

Our artists get inspiration from their surroundings, from nature and their homes. Some of the designs have a traditional origin. On occasion, our artists will ask for new ideas and inspiration from our office and we will supply images that could potentially be turned into a new design. Tintsaba also collaborates with international artists and designers to develop new ranges of products.

5. We noticed that the names of the colors are very interesting like Poolside, Safari, Summer Love, Mother of Pearl, etc. Could you please share some meanings of the names?

Many of our colors are inspired by native African nature. For example, the Safari color comes from a trip taken in the world-famous national park, Kruger National Park in South Africa, 30 minutes from Tintsaba. The olive of the scrub bush land, the gold of the Mopani trees–these red of the earth, and white and cream thorns on the trees, the colors are the essence of where we come from. Kalahari is another example. It was inspired by a photo of the setting sun over the desert. Summer Love is full of bright, warm, summery colors, almost like a candy box. The name came from the famous Grease song. Our designer felt the hope, love and joy of the colors reflected in the name.

6. What are your hopes and future plans for the field?

Tintsaba will continue in our founder's footsteps, where innovation and experiment are a constant. We are planning to make the baskets more easily accessible to the collector and home decorator. We want to share our hearts, our stories and art with the world. Together we can weave a better life.

^ Baskets: Blossom

"Blossom" is a selection of baskets in the Blossom color.

Materials: sisal, grass

"Our artists get inspiration from their surroundings, from nature and their homes. Some of the designs have a traditional origin."

^ Basket: Kalahari (upper left)

“Kalahari” is a 31cm Gallery Grade basket in the Kalahari color.

Materials: sisal, grass

^ Mop (upper right)

“Mop” is a Gallery Grade basket in the Mother of Pearl color.

Materials: sisal, grass

^ Basket: Earth (bottom)

“Earth” is a 31cm Gallery Grade basket in the Earth color.

Materials: sisal, grass

Myriam Balaÿ | France

· **Myriam Balaÿ** ·

Myriam Balaÿ is a maker. After graduating with a degree in industrial product design, Myriam entered the textile world and had memorable experiences in haute couture (Chanel, Dior,) designing textile products for the company "Du proche et du lointain" and serving as the co-founder and artistic manager of the Copirates brand.

Twenty years ago, she visited India where she had set up a weaving production for large textile pieces with a technique close to Ikat. The system allowed her to test a lot of things in terms of colors and materials. As an autodidact, Myriam was trained in weaving techniques and her pieces have been very successful. Today, Myriam has changed tools and miniaturized her loom. "It's portable. It's convenient. I take it everywhere. I can even work on the train and in the car. These bracelets are like miniatures of these big pieces and they serve to create color palettes. But, ultimately, I weave as would any weaver who lives on the banks of the Nile River."

One of the most striking features of her work is that it's handmade. Everything has a story. Myriam's newest endeavor is Bracelets Loom, launched in 2014 and sold internationally. In her home studio, her loom is set up, ready to weave her threads into one-of-a-kind creations.

1. You have designed textiles for fashion brands like Chanel and Dior. What's the most memorable creation you have ever made?

When collaborating with haute couture brands, I worked on material manufacturing and pattern design, rather than assembling and finishing the whole collections. And because of that, I don't think there is a piece of work that I consider memorable. What I got from such experience, even more memorable than the style work done on computers in Paris studio, is that all the prototyping work was done in the mountains of Forez (Loire), far from Paris. The whole team (graphic designer, weaver, haute couture trainee) settled in a Jacquard weaving workshop and I was then associated with the entire creative process on the loom. The team had an incredible choice of threads, a variety of colors and the ability to experiment without any restrictions. It was that kind of immersive work style, paired with many available materials and tools that made this experience beautiful. My goal there was essentially to work on Chanel's dresses. And now when I meet a woman who wears a Chanel dress, I tell myself that it may be made from a fabric that I helped to weave. It makes me happy and proud.

2. Could you please share with us the story of your Bracelets Loom? What or who inspires you to create them?

For weaving, I get inspiration from everything. Nature is important to me and it inspires me to complete all the photos I made during my study in fine arts. Nature is an infinite collection of colors, shapes and materials. When I mean nature, it can be a very broad thing. It can also be a corner of an urban landscape or a flower placed on a coffee table or a passing landscape on a train trip. It represents a reverie or a moment when we concentrate on the detail of an object. Flowers are one of my favorite subjects. I'm fortunate to have a chance to collaborate with a very beautiful magazine for a few years, so I can further emphasize and express my relationship with nature and flowers and colors.

Another great source of inspiration, especially for technique and know-how, is related to my Indian experience—the large abstract woven pieces and the materials. In India, I learned that everything is possible. It's that spirit that prevailed when I launched the LOOMs series. The idea was to create a miniature work on great Indian textile pieces. I've been working on woven collection for more than 20 years and it's like a link in

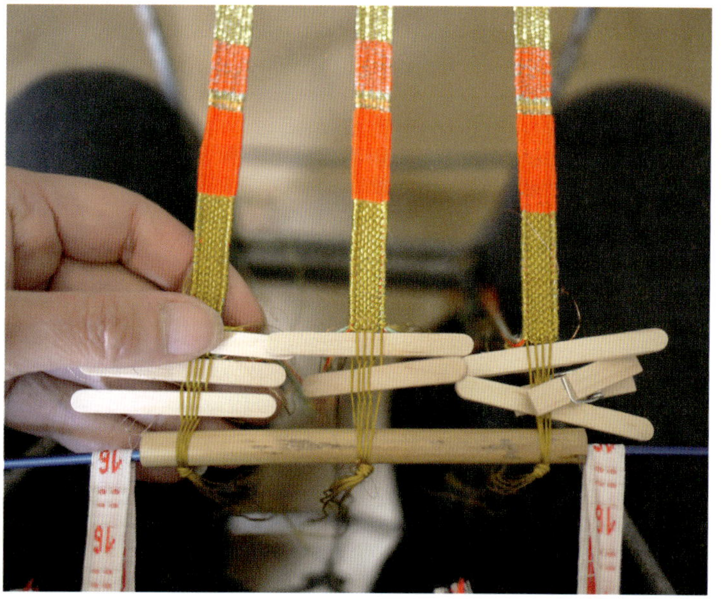

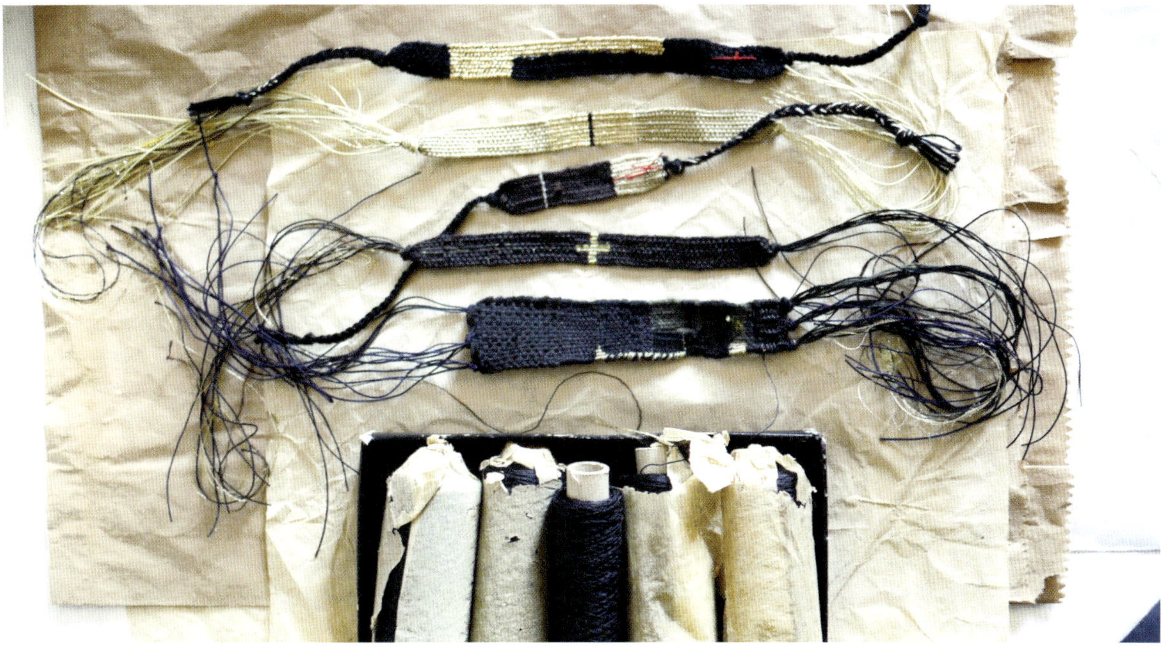

time and space. Initially, I didn't want to make a bracelet. The collection just naturally became a sort of fashion accessory and I knew it was necessary that this miniature work should have a function and meet future customers. I am not a pure dreamer: like all creators, I need my work to earn a living.

The pattern of the repetitive cross on the LOOMs refers to the first textile piece I wove in India. This cross is like a pooja to me. In India, when a weaving loom is installed and ready for use, the weaver says a prayer and makes ritual offerings (pooja) before operating it. To respect this rite, I made a cross on my LOOMs collections. The name of my bracelets comes simply from the English words of "loom" or "handloom."

3. The retro-styled colors of your bracelets is very special. Do you have a method for choosing color palettes?

To create my palettes of color, I study the collection of old threads that I sourced from various flea markets in France and Europe. I spend a lot of time looking for threads that match my work and meet my desires. I love doing it so very much. I find it easy to mix older threads with some new ones. I also match precious materials with raw materials, for example, jeans cloth with golden threads. The indigo LOOMs with golden threads is one of my classic bracelets.

4. Besides Bracelets Loom, you also work in different fields of art like making paper lamps. What's the commonality between paper art and fiber art?

Paper and fabric are both made of cotton. I only use paper made from cotton fiber for my lamps. I know how to use paper for my weavings very well because the two materials are naturally linked. And I use fabric all the time. This is a kind of material I particularly like because fabric matches almost everything. I like its flexibility and lightness. I'm glad to use such material for something light and bright like the lamps.

5. What has been your greatest challenge to date? How did you conquer it?

Making my customers understand that it takes time to weave my bracelets is one of my biggest challenges. I need a rather long manufacturing time because I do everything myself and I work alone. After all, I'm not a machine.

Traditional craft is sometimes misunderstood, although it's still appreciated by many. People must understand that for an artisan, there is no difference between life and work. It's a work life that we choose willingly, a life full of creation and happiness.

Bracelets LOOM

All Bracelets LOOM are handmade in Myriam Balaÿ's studio in the south of France.

Tools: portable looms
Materials: linen, silk, cotton, hemp, vintage threads

^ Bracelet LOOM N ° 96 (upper)

Tools: portable looms
Materials: linen, silk, cotton, hemp, vintage threads

"Traditional craft is sometimes misunderstood, although it's still appreciated by many. People must understand that for an artisan, there is no difference between life and work."

Caroline Kaszak | France

· Caroline Kaszak ·

Caroline Kaszak is an artist and maker based in France. To her, weaving was an integral part of her childhood. She was first exposed to weaving in her father's workshops. The weaving was industrial, punctuated by the great automated looms. However, at that time, her artistic experience was related to photography and drawing. With a degree in arts and communication, she worked initially on the establishment of art exhibitions and concerts. But the artistic milieu has always been present in one way or another. Her arrival in Cévennes, France marked the beginning of a change of life. In 2014, she returned to the textile world with a renewed interest in weaving. In constant experimentation, she weaves with other materials, integrating wood and the plants that surround her or applying other techniques such as embroidery and vegetable dyes. She set up her company, Woodhappen, in 2016, creating wooden furniture and weavings that reappear the landscapes in the form of pleating. Braiding and weaving with natural fibers, Caroline creates artworks and furniture providing a modern takes in the ancient craft of seat weaving.

1. Please share with us your weaving process from conception to creation.

I explore the simple gesture of the work of rope and thread. I weave them and braid them to make works of art, accessories or even furniture. I like to offer a modern touch to ancient crafts. Usually, I begin by drawing the patterns and shapes that I want to incorporate into my weaving. This is the stage of pure creation. The techniques I then use are a mixture of weaving and braiding. I wanted to free myself from the loom. I weave and braid directly on a wooden frame that I make or recover. The materials most often used are natural fibers such as flax, cotton or hemp or recycled materials.

2. You have tried to weave by combining different materials. There must be many challenges during the process. How do you conquer them?

I use many natural and raw materials. Different materials have different proteins like the roughness of hemp and jute, the softness of cotton and the natural elegance of linen. Each fiber is woven differently. I also used thin sheets of wood that I cut into thin strips. The wood is woven and braided delicately and each species has its peculiarity. The chestnut tree, for example, is easily split. It is a job that is still close to the old profession, that of a basket maker. In the Cévennes and elsewhere, people can find baskets braided with thin blades of chestnut wood. It was by meeting craftsmen and discovering the techniques that I was able to introduce other materials and then appropriate them. I am also attentive to weaving techniques that we can find in other cultures, such as raffia weaving among the Batéké in Congo. I also collaborate with a painter, Cécile Guérard, who uses a particular technique for her paintings. I weave and braid his paintings. There are many difficulties and it is work for four hands. Successive attempts and failures do the rest. I love challenges. All these experiences require time, to excel and not to lose sight of the finality to which one inspires.

3. We noticed that you also do wooden marquetry. What's the most interesting aspect of wooden marquetry? Did you get inspiration from wooden marquetry while weaving?

I keep exploring the world of wood by working in parallel with modern marquetry. I like to create patterns

using recycled wood or wood from a reasoned logging operation. My creations are handcrafted and eco-friendly. I create paintings and furniture. As for the textiles, I am attracted to the natural shades and patterns that I brought with me from my travels. The creation of the patterns is close to that of weaving. My marquetry paintings are comparable to pieces of fabric and you can find points on textiles that look like the chevron stitch.

4. You introduce some weaving techniques on your website. What does sharing these techniques mean to you?

I think the internet has brought us a lot. Today, everyone has access to everything with just a few clicks. It is easy to exchange ideas, even with people on the other side of the world. This accessibility creates vocations. It also enables others to appropriate techniques and to promote evolution. I have developed several tutorials on weaving with a table loom allowing everyone to start a wall weaving from scratch. This is a very interesting exercise. The most difficult thing is to put oneself in the shoes of someone who has never touched a loom, and to develop a suitable pedagogy and to have a precise vision of one's work and of the techniques one uses.

5. The pattern of your work is unique. How did you find your artistic style?

I have plenty of inspiration. On the artistic level, I was influenced by artists like Sheila Hicks, of course, Peter Collingwood, Olga de Amaral and Judith Scott. I also draw the world around me, the world of skateboarding and street art. The shapes I create are inspired by the architecture of buildings. I am very sensitive to imagery and to what I feel. I love the contrast of woven straight and urban shapes with natural and raw materials. I've lived part of my life in remote and wild places, but also large cities and I need both to find a balance. My creations reflect this duality, this balance.

6. What other hobbies or passions do you have besides weaving?

I grew up in the skateboarding culture and my lifestyle is shaped by that. It's an inspiring, multi-faceted background. Photography is also very important to me. I got my first camera when I was 13 years old. I always carry it with me and I can't stay away from it. I need to capture moments, a light or a face. I also draw a lot. It is vital to create something. Nature is also a prominent place like the Cévennes in the South of France. That's where I recharge my batteries.

Cord and Wood

"Cord and Wood" is an association of wood and fibers. On one side, it's maple and on the other side, oak.

Tools: wooden needle

˄ Tableau Braided Architecture 0.4

"Tableau Braided Architecture 0.4" is a textile table woven with geometric shapes inspired by architecture.

› Stool

Each piece is hand woven with a unique array of patterns and colors. The frame is an old stool that has been reworked and sanded.

Tools: wooden needle
Materials: humble old stool, cotton and linen cords

Christina Christensen | Denmark

· Christina Christensen ·

Christina Christensen is a designer and art weaver from Denmark. She is also the founder and co-owner of FRIDAJOHS design studio, a multidisciplinary design studio that does tailor-made design, illustrations and graphic design projects for many different companies. For many years, Christina has worked in the commercial and industrial design world where craftsmanship and artistic works are a low priority—it is more about fast business. It was not until she became self-employed with her design studio in 2016 that she began to seriously experiment with other kinds of processes and artistic approaches to design and crafts. Christina combines traditional craftsmanship with unconventional materials. Her idea of weaving with plants started as a fascination with common plants. One of her interests is also to photograph the most common occurrences in nature in a new way. At one point, a little idea started to sprout and she began to imagine how very common and accessible plants would look in a weaving.

"It is fascinating to work with the combination of the natural material and the loom as a tool. It gives some obstructions when the natural dried plants have a special fixed defined form together with the thread, which can be modulated, stretched and yet clamped in the loom. The interaction gives a rhythm and a special visual language, which differs widely from plant to plant. This rhythm is alluring and makes me curious," she said. Christina has always been in love with the work of the hands and, in textiles, she will continue to experiment with alternative materials and combine them with old and new techniques.

1. You have many identities—a visual artist, fashion and interior designer, brand manager, art director and photographer. Which identity is your favorite one? What did you learn from working in different fields?

I have always been very curious about creative work and process. I've always been aware that at some point I was going to be a self-employed designer—I just had doubts in which direction (I'm still finding my way, but I'm getting closer). That is why I have been very open-minded and ready to learn about new aspects in the field of creative business. It has provided me with many exciting and evolving projects, and has given me more experience than any education could give me. All my identities help me to create a better and more coherent result. I love being a part of the whole process of designing and building something new and, therefore, my favorite identity in my professional work is designer—I want to be the project manager who also has her fingers in the creative and creating process.

2. Please share with us your weaving process from conception to creation.

I have a very visual mind. I find inspiration everywhere. My artistic development takes place almost unconsciously like visualizations in my head. I combine a small glimpse of inspiration and ideas into an inner picture. It's unnecessary to create physical sketches. Often my motivation starts with material or technique that I want to experiment with. Sometimes an idea evolves on a single day and I need to bring it to life immediately. Other times, it can take weeks or months to combine the perfect ideas—and even though the idea is clear when I start, the process is always changed by new inputs and directions. I like to get a clean expression.

The creative process is quite different in my professional job as a designer when I draw sketches by hand and on computer. I create mood boards or collages and explore possible materials and seek knowledge and inspiration in books and online. When the idea is formed, I draw and thoroughly describe details before submitting the project for approval and later for production.

3. We notice that you usually collect plants from nature and combine them into your fiber works. How do you deal with the plants after collecting? Could you give us an example?

Collecting natural plants and using them for weaving requires time and patience and also depends on which plants you are collecting and what expression you want to achieve. In connection with my rye-weave, I waited

Fragile weave with dried lunaria.

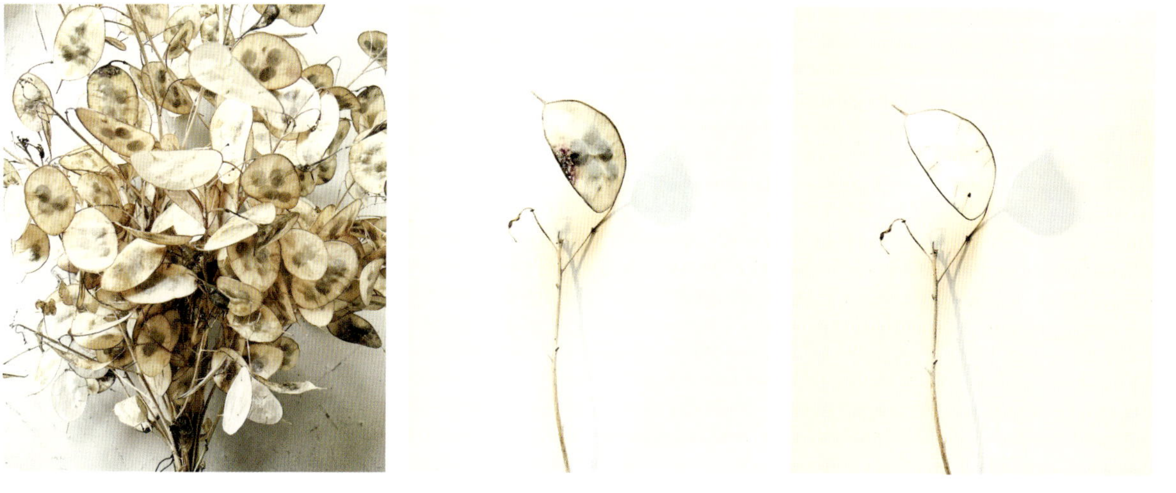

until the end of the season before I collected straw at a local field. Rye is the tallest grain crop in Denmark. It's approximately 50–150 cm high and it provides a long piece of straw to work with. Then, I bundled them up and hanged them with their heads down in my dark garage. They dried for a few weeks before I started weaving. You would think the straw would be fragile and easy to break, but it was surprisingly durable and easier to work with than I expected.

4. The work Lunaria is woven by combining fiber with Lunaria. Mostly the dried flowers are easily broken. Was it difficult to weave this work? What's the most difficult aspect of the process?

My mother-in-law gave me a big bouquet of Lunaria. I think it is a very beautiful dried plant and, therefore, I used it as inspiration decor in my studio. After a while, it suddenly occurred to me that the combination of weaving and Lunaria could be very interesting. However, it was clear that I could not weave with Lunaria alone, although it has been dogma for me so far only to use fiber threads for warp. I started with a prototype where I found a cotton and linen blend that had the same shine and elegance as dried Lunaria. Although dried plants can seem very fragile and easy to break, they also have strength, if treated properly. Of course, quite a few broke along the way—also because I had to try several times before I had the right recipe and combination for the final Lunaria weave. It was a challenge and a very slow process to weave this piece, but enchanting to look at along the way. And, fortunately, my mother-in-law had much more dried Lunaria in stock.

5. The style of your fiber works is reminiscent of the beauty in nature. Is that the feeling you want to share with the audience? What do you want to express through your works?

I think I want to communicate that everything does not need to be super-fast. If you are patient and attentive, beautiful details appear from things you might take for granted. I am professionally shaped by an industrial and commercial mindset where everything has to be perfect and produced in 10,000 identical copies—and for a long time, I wanted to challenge that mindset. I do this by working very slowly with my hands and with materials that can only be harvested at the right time once a year and then the plants also need to dry and change in character before I even start working with them. I would like to highlight the quality and beauty of plants and nature that we do not necessarily notice. And then I think that we should be more aware of the beauty of nature, which, me, is a common language and a shared responsibility around the globe.

No Straw Shortener

These two weavings were exhibited at "Biennale for Crafts and Design 2019" in Copenhagen. The work shows two ordinary crops from Denmark in a new and relevant context that brings us close to something we often see from a distance. It is a comment about our shared language through nature and the importance of a shared responsibility to take care of nature. The rye is sourced from a nearby field, close to the home of Christina in Odder, Denmark—and the reeds are harvested at a local beach called Kysing Beach.

Tools: Lervad handloom
Materials: rye, reeds, cotton, linen, brass

Rope–Let the Material Speak

One of these weavings is dark and the other is light. It is an experiment with used rope. The rope is divided and then weaved into another purpose and context. In the process, the waves of the rope have formed a tactile surface, which catches the light in a unique way.

Tools: Lervad handloom
Materials: recycled rope, recycled camel-wool, brass

Catriona Pollard | Australia

· Catriona Pollard ·

Catriona Pollard is a sculptural fiber artist. Her unique sculptural work offers glimpses of shape-shifting natural forms, from unnoticed branches, leaves and seedpods into works that investigate human being's connection to the natural world. Her sculptural abstractive landscapes were made by using foraged and discarded plant material with traditional basketry and assemblage techniques. By transforming organic material into sculptures, she is investigating the battle humans have between controlling nature and seeing ourselves in harmony with it.

Her work adds a contemporary layer to the ancient art form of weaving, which is often dismissed as a functional craft. Her work allows the audience to review their assumptions about craft and its potential in art. When they see her work, it forces them to see beyond their concept of basketry. Through this reinterpretation of nature, her work expresses a concept that we should actively see nature as part of us, rather than simply an object that has no meaning or spirit. This investigation also leads to a reflection on our inner landscape and questioning control versus harmony within our lives.

Catriona has had numerous solo exhibitions, and has exhibited extensively in selected and group exhibitions. She has been short-listed for numerous art awards, and teaches a range of basketry workshops in Australia and internationally. Her work is profiled across major art and design media, and is featured nationally in galleries, high-end design spaces and private collections.

1. Your works are in many different shapes. How do you get inspiration and transform your ideas into such expressive sculptures?

Nature is my main inspiration as it is where I find beauty, peace and creativity. For me, the power of natural beauty energizes me. It makes my soul sing. Growing up in the outback with summers at the beach, taking part in school holiday camping and walking through national parks has resulted in a deep connection with the natural world around me. As I walk through the bush tracks around my home town of Sydney and its harbor, inspiration presents itself. I see a fallen tree with the roots exposed and an idea for a sculpture is illuminated. Or as I wade through the rock pools, the shape of the water against the rocks becomes an idea for a sculpture. Basketry to me is about seeing the potential, which may not be readily apparent. You may walk past a fallen branch and not even notice it, but I may see the beginnings of a sculpture. It's pure joy to pick up a vine, stick or seed pod and imagine what they could become. I use materials to tell my stories and they represent every facet of me. I use nature and basketry as a way to connect with people that goes beyond physical beauty, but touches them in a personal and profound way.

2. What types of fibers do you most often use? Why? Will different materials affect the outcome of your works?

Right at the beginning of my practice, it was the connection with nature and creativity that I wanted to deepen, so I made a purposeful decision to use discarded, foraged, found or gifted plant materials, and to avoid bought and synthetic materials. Finding the material is constant. It's not simply going online to order material. I spend days in the bush or walking through my suburb collecting and drying and getting the material ready to use. I also need to know when material can be collected. For example, in early spring, I collect the falling jacaranda stalks and summer is the best time for the Bangalow palm inflorescence. I use many types of organic plant fibers, but I mainly use Australian natives including Bangalow palm inflorescence, five-leaf water vine and Wonga Wonga Vine.

3. Please tell us a bit about your chosen techniques and how you use them.

While I'm in awe of them, the precise patterns of many of the basket-making techniques don't appeal to me. It's the form and structure I'm drawn to explore and the techniques that allow me to do this are random weave and twining. For twining, the weaving is done with two elements woven simultaneously around spokes. The weaving elements cross between the spokes for half or a full turn. For the beginner, it's good to use different materials for the spoke and weaver, although I prefer to use the same materials. There are several ways to start a twined basket and I specialize in the "bundle start." For random weaving, there are many different ways to do it. The common element is that the spoke and the weaver are the same, so you are creating a conversation between the two elements. As there is no specific pattern, this can be a hard technique as you are constantly reviewing your next weave.

4. You have done weaving sessions with different artists. Which session did you think was the most impressive?

I have learned the techniques and approaches from wonderful artists. However, the most impressive teacher is the materials I use. Weaving by using organic material is about listening to what it wants to be. I may have an idea about what I'm going to create and then I'll pick up the material and start. The material decides what it wants to become. You always need to learn from the material. As I'm working with plant fibers, sometimes the branches and vines don't behave in the way that I want them to. One time, I found beautiful branches covered in moss and spent hours trying to make them into a sculpture. I gave up in the end. But that's the beauty of it—no two pieces will turn out the same and it's the unpredictability of these pieces that make them unique and special.

5. You also teach. Is that an interesting experience? What do you want to bring to your students?

I think that once you get to a certain level, it's important to share your knowledge. We have seen a noticeable resurgence in creating traditional crafts in the past few years. I think it's the result of how virtual our lives have become and how busy we all seem to be. People are looking for arts and crafts that reconnect them with slower, traditional creative experiences. I believe basketry helps us slow down, quiets the mind and puts us in touch with our inner wisdom. All of my works are based on connecting my hands with my heart through nature. If you come to any of my workshops, you'll understand that I teach in this way, too. It's so much more than learning a basketry technique. It's connecting to age-old practices and using basketry to uncover our creativity.

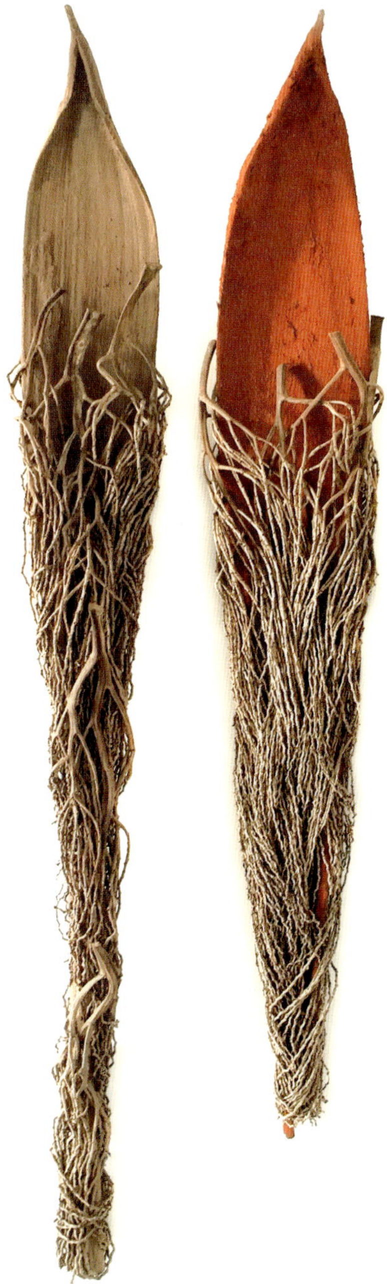

^ Cocos Palm and Bangalow Palm

Cocos palm is native to Brazil and Catriona uses the sheath that protects the flower that falls to the ground. In these sculptures, the weaving material is the Australian native Bangalow palm. She uses the inflorescence, which is the complete flower head of the palm. It grows along the east coast of Australia. The inflorescence dries on the palm and falls to the ground.

Tools: metal cutters
Materials: Bangalow palm, palm sheath, camp fire ash of mulga wood, red sand

› Twining

Twining is a specific basketry technique with two elements woven simultaneously around a spoke. Catriona uses this technique on a variety of natural material.

Materials: cumbungi, tea tree, Bangalow palm inflorescence, rattan, cumbungi

Totems for the Trees

"Totems for the Trees" represents the need to hold sacred our link to forests, bush land and trees. Our ancestry is so closely connected to the earth and the vines, leaves and plants that grow from it. Here are Catriona's totems to honor and worship the earth beneath our feet and the new growth that can emerge from it.

Materials: willow, rattan, dodder, dragon fruit leaves, birch, clay, ash, charcoal

Taiwan Yuan-Li Handiwork Association | Miaoli, Taiwan, China

· **Taiwan Yuan-Li Handiwork Association** ·

Rush weaving is a traditional handmade art dating back to the Qing Dynasty of China and it has a rich culture and history. The Taiwan Yuan-Li Handiwork Association is an association aiming to preserve the craft of rush grass weaving, cultivate craftsmen and innovate products made of rush grasses. In the past, at Yuan Li, rush weaving was an industry for women. In each family, every woman weaved rush bunches one after another whether she was a daughter, a daughter-in-law, a mother or a mother-in-law. With the establishment of the Taiwan Yuan-Li Handiwork Association, the women in Yuan Li town were encouraged to continue the tradition. The underlying structure of rush grass industries, based on traditional sustainability and innovative design, enables modern people to appreciate the natural beauty of rush grass craft. Additionally, to promote traditional rush weaving skill, the Taiwan Yuan-Li Handiwork Association has sponsored many activities. Meanwhile, teachers and students in the design department have been dispatched to learn about weaving with rush grasses, so that more young designers become familiar with the traditional craft. Since 2006, the association has sponsored the Rush-Love Craft Award, aiming to improve the creativity of artisans and to energize the traditional rush weaving craft through cross-field cooperation between designers and artisans. The Taiwan Yuan-Li Handiwork Association is reluctant to see this meaningful handicraft fade away and hopes to improve the sustainable industrial development of rush weaving.

1. Could you please tell us more about rush grasses? Why do you prefer using rush grasses as your major weaving material?

Rush, commonly known as mat grass, has different usages and characteristics due to different planting seasons. Mat grass of the first season is called "early rush" or "spring rush." It is suitable for making big products because of its long length. The second season of the rush grass is called "yunzai rush," which is stronger compared to the other seasons. Artisans prefer to use it to make high-end hat. The third season of the rush grass is called "third winter-rush." It's usually used for rope material because of its rough texture. The rush growing in about a 10 km area between the north of the Da'an River and the south of the Yuanli River has the finest texture, the greatest toughness, the highest water absorption and the richest fragrance. All these features help the rush survive dividing, beetling, buffeting and so on. The users of rush appreciate the skin-friendly features and strong fragrance.

2. You collect and dry the rush grass yourself. What do you need to pay attention to during the process?

In the past, every rice-growing family always had an exclusive place for growing rush in the field. The rush growing made the family self-sufficient. That's because the rush is triple cropping with seedling during the first season and naturally growing in the following two seasons as the root—"vitality origin"—remains. Although rush grows fast and is easy to plant, the high-quality rush is tougher to grow. It requires water and fertilizer, and the care and harvesting need to be conducted by hand. Finally, the rush with the brightest color and the highest quality can be produced. Right now, since the rush industry and the number of rush farmers is declining, we need to learn how to grow rush by hand. In this way, we can ensure the proper quality and quantity of rush.

3. All of your works are hand-woven. Is it time-consuming? Why do you prefer weaving by hand?

For Yuanli people, the fine and delicate pattern of rush work, and the soft and tough texture have special meaning. With rush craft, you can not only feel the kind-hearted and creative nature of our Taiwan ancestors, but you also can appreciate the design elements of each work. The traditions of the local Taiwanese people have not disappeared. Instead, we see them in the crafts of everyday life.

4. As time passes, some traditional techniques of rush grass weaving have become hard to find. Fortunately, we can still find the traces of those masterly techniques in your products. Was it difficult to restore the weaving techniques? How did you do it?

Though the rush weaving industry is fading, our artisans are still doing on this traditional work. They are working hard to record each technique and every weaving step. We also teach rush weaving skills. We are also offering certifications for rush weaving artisans.

5. As the development of machines continues, more and more traditional crafts are gradually disappearing. Why and how do you want to revive rush grass weaving and make it a new industry?

Rush weaving has a rich local culture and historical meaning. The rush industry has formed a unique local industrial ecology chain. The overall production and sales of rush weaving are structured by these various networks. In a way, it connects the common memories of Yuanli people. As people visit the association, they share their childhood memories of the rush weaving artistry. Since the artisans in the workshop are mostly from Yuanli, their memories of rush weaving come from their lives and their memories. This is where the cultural root belongs. We are reluctant to see this meaningful handicraft of traditional local culture disappear.

6. The style of traditional crafts is not widely accepted in modern times. What would you do to meet this challenge? Have you made any innovations?

Tradition has its beauty, while innovation has its flavor. In earlier times, rush works showed simplicity and pureness. In the new era, rush weaving works have been innovated. Nowadays, rush weaving products are becoming more diverse, covering all the aspects of modern life, such as slippers, helmet linings, pencil boxes, notebooks, bookmarks, magnetic pet toys, cell phone bags, iPad bags, handbags, lamps, baby supplies, etc. New ideas are introduced. The repeated dialogues between the delicate rush weaving skills and the different materials and shapes, present a new beginning for rush weaving. Besides its useful functions, you can also appreciate the traditional, delicate and rich patterns.

Simple Life Series

The "Simple Life Series" combines different weaving techniques such as bamboo weaving, fishing net weaving and so on, which is unlike the traditional delicate weaving techniques. The rough weaving style not only expresses the beauty of rush grass, but also combines vegetable tanning, which is a tanning method, for the bag's handle. The colors will change when it's used. Having this design series at home brings you a sense of warmth. This series of works is simple and cozy, while providing people with a multifunctional and decorative storage design.

Materials: Cyperus malaccensis, vegetable-tanned leather

Esthetic of the Rush Weaving Pattern

In the early days, rush weaving works were mats, hats, cushions and so on. However, the most impressive part of rush weaving was the vivid patterns formed by the bunch cross. It may be the simple bottom I, the firm bottom II or the netting pattern, which the light may penetrate. Based on the fundamental patterns above, more patterns are created, such as the pineapple pattern, feather pattern, rhombus pattern, plum blossom pattern, net pattern, copper coin pattern, purslane flower pattern, turtle shell pattern, etc. All the patterns are the result from hard work and every detail represents their insistence for quality.

Materials: Cyperus malaccensis

PHOTOGRAPHY: **Brenton McGeachie (photo on page 198).**

Sally Blake | Australia

· Sally Blake ·

Sally Blake is a visual artist based in Canberra, Australia. She completed her doctorate degree in textiles at the Australian National University in 2015. She works across different textile, sculptural and paper-based mediums and techniques. Sally's practice is concerned with visualizing the complex interconnections between the human and natural worlds through textile and paper-based media to examine the synergies, connections and tensions between humans and nature in her art practice. To reveal these connections, she works with natural processes and materials such as plant dyes in the creation of artworks. She is particularly concerned with cycles of death and renewal and regeneration as well as finding the points where transformations may take place. In her contemporary drawings and textiles, these natural cycles are explored as well as the consequences of their undoing. She feels deeply about disconnections in the human understanding of the natural world, which results in environmental crises.

1. Could you please tell us a bit about your research? Why did you start it?

My Ph.D. research was practice-led and, through it, I explored the relationship between my inner world and the outer world of nature. This focus developed from my concern about human-led ecological crises such as climate change and flora and fauna extinctions. A methodology based on Donald Winnicott's theory of potential space was used to explore this relationship. Potential space is a state of mind that allows for inner and outer reality to be negotiated with an attitude of openness and playfulness. These connections were explored using textile and drawing-based works that articulated and recorded the patterns and transformations that emerged between self and nature in potential space. Through experiences and collaborations with nature, the visual research took several forms including weaving, piecing, plant dyeing, drawings made with rain and burns, stitching and piercing paper. The research extended Winnicott's psychodynamic concept by exploring its relevance for understanding the relationship between self and nature. Several art-making methodologies were presented as ways to understand and investigate the synergies, connections, and tensions between humans and nature.

2. You have developed a eucalyptus dye database. We really appreciate that. Was it difficult? Why did you want to do this project?

In Australia, we have over 800 species of eucalyptus, with each species giving a unique dye from their leaves and bark. The eucalyptus dyes are substantive plant dyes and they are pretty resistant to fading in light or washing. This makes them an important plant-dye source in Australia and in other countries where eucalyptus are now grown. I wanted to create a free and easily accessible resource of the eucalyptus dyes for artists and others to use. The dye colors reveal another aspect of this iconic Australian species. My research was in collaboration with the Australian National Botanical Gardens where the rangers helped me to collect all the leaves and bark. Processing the leaves from 230 species and the barks from 100 was a large task. I had to use consistent recipes for each dye so the results from different species could be compared. I used three different fibers: wool, silk and linen to collect the dyes as each fiber takes the dyes differently. Additionally, I used three mordants: alum, iron and copper for the color changes. In total, I made more than 1,300 colors.

 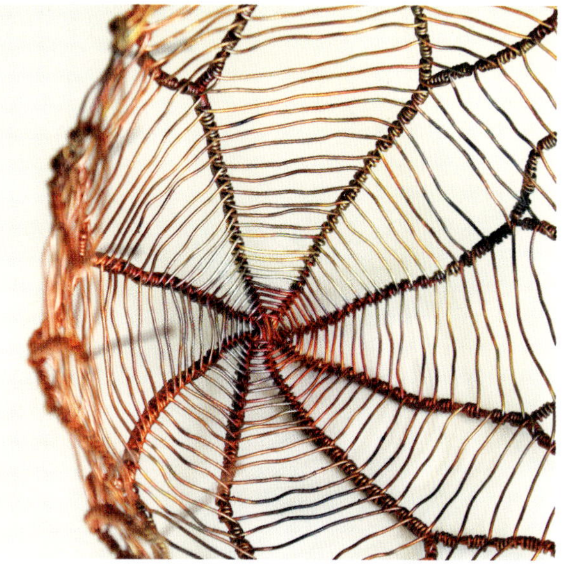

The other big part of this project was photographing all the results to post online. I corrected every dye color in Photoshop and create my online eucalyptus dye database with all the results, plus recipes and information about the dyes.

3. You do your dyeing yourself. Could you please share with us some knowledge about plant dyes? What is the most difficult part of the dyeing process?

For me, the most wonderful thing about plant dyes is their unpredictability, but this can be a source of frustration for some people. Plant dyes are never totally repeatable as each dye color is an indicator of the constantly changing conditions the plant lives in. Factors such as rainfall, the soil and other biophysical factors affecting the plant will influence the dye colors.

I don't think plant dyes are difficult to work with, but the art of using these dyes requires knowledge that deepens with time and experience as the dyer become more sensitive to and familiar with the materials used. People who are impatient or scared to experiment will find this difficult.

Working with plant dyes allows me to discover more about the place where I live by unlocking and discovering the otherwise unseen colors that plants produce as dyes. These colors reveal a layer of complexity, beauty and wonder in the natural world that is otherwise hidden from view.

4. What type of weaving materials do you often use? Why? Will different materials affect the outcome of your works?

The main materials I use for weaving are wire, copper, silver, aluminum and plant-dyed yarns, including wool, silk, linen and hemp. I started using wire to give my works structural strength and I like that works made from wire can look quite delicate and fragile while also having strength. I use the plant-dyed yarns as a record of place and the landscape where I collected the plant materials to make the dyes.

One thing that always surprises me with a slow technique like basket weaving is that the final work can look quite different from how I imagined it would be. The materials I use influence the outcomes and seem to have a mind of their own.

5. The "vein" of the work "Commonwealth of Breath" is really amazing like the network of capillaries in one's body. How long did it take to create this work? How did you achieve such an authentic effect?

It's hard to remember exactly how long this work took to make. I tend to forget once the work is done, but probably about a month. To get an authentic effect with this work, I studied medical illustrations of lungs and the bronchial tree. It was a good challenge and pushed my making skills as I manipulated the wire to look like the branching bronchial system. I had to be constantly problem solving to find ways to mimic the structures.

^ Held Mysteries

Sally uses her sensitivity with materials to create artworks that explore eucalyptus dyes on a range of natural fibers and threads. The small baskets have been made by using a range of threads dyed from the colors of one eucalyptus species. Using plant dyes is a mysterious process emerging between the plant materials and human intervention. Many eucalyptus give unexpected results such as bright oranges and reds on wool.

Materials: copper-wire, eucalyptus-dyed wool, silk, hemp

C.ficifolia (dwarf orange) leaves

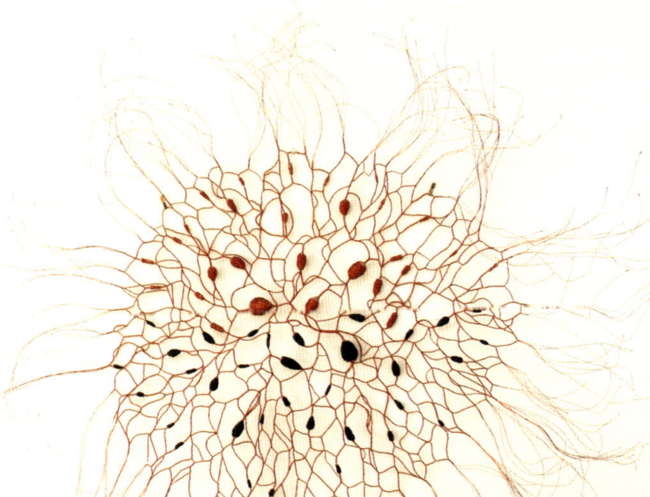

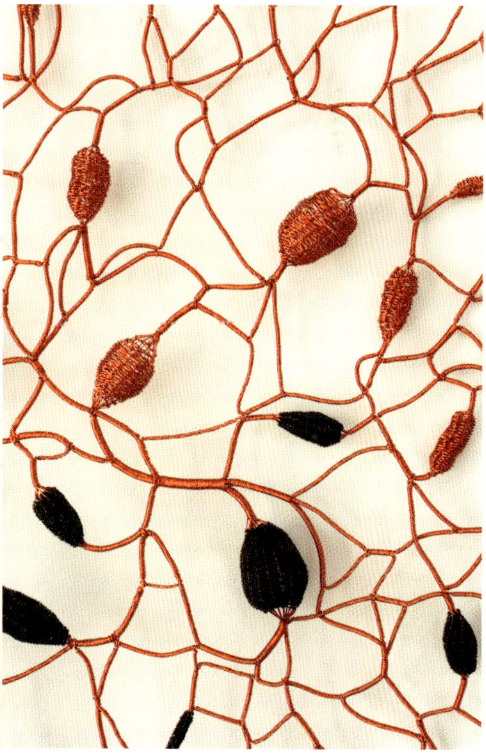

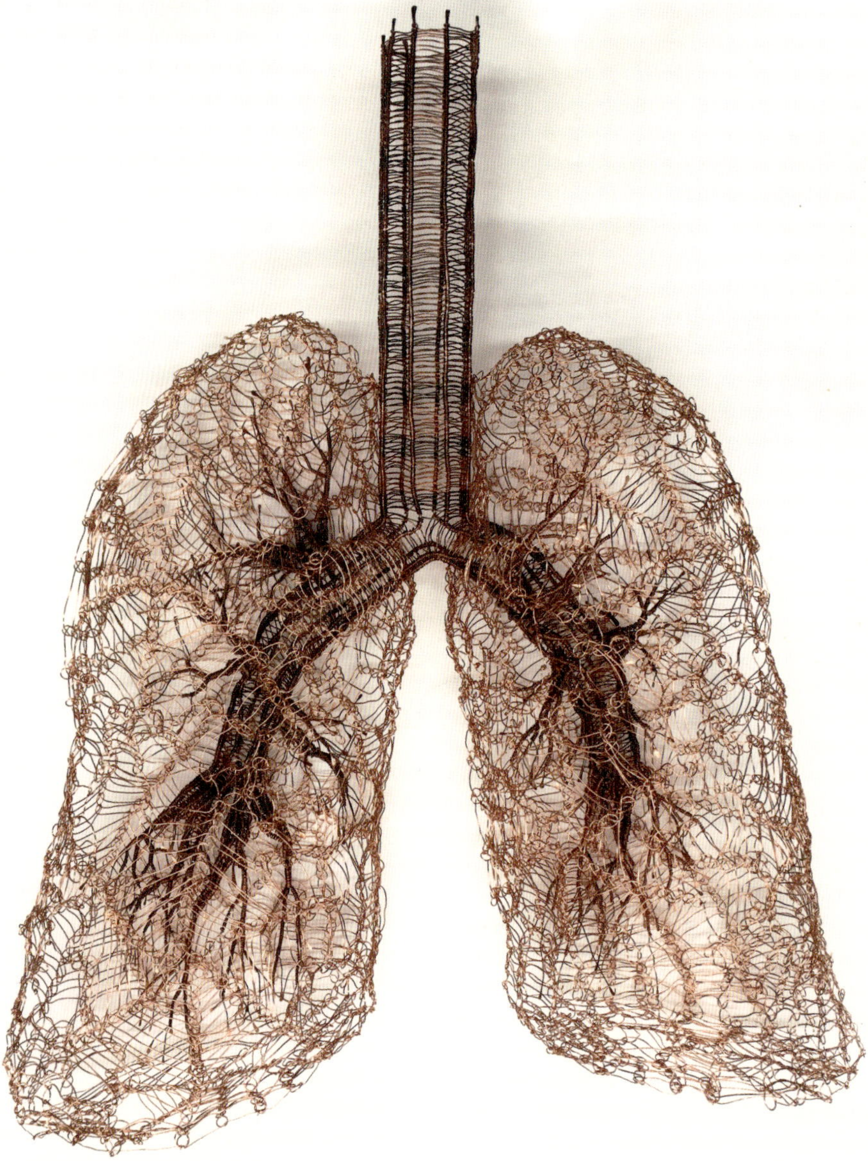

^ Commonwealth of Breath

"Commonwealth of Breath" is made from looped and copper wire. Environmental philosopher David Abram coined the phrase, "commonwealth of breath" to examine the atmosphere that connects humans with the rest of the planet. This work is a representation of human lungs. With every breath, in and out, we are relating to and connecting with other living creatures. Our inner worlds and outer worlds are linked. The looping technique used for creating the lungs creates an intermeshed surface, which is a metaphor for the interconnected nature of all living and non-living things.

Materials: patinated copper wire

Coiled baskets, twined baskets, copper-wire works and woven tapestries.

PHOTOGRAPHY: Brenton McGeachie (photos on page 206–207).

"My main advice would be to find the ideas that you want to explore in and through your artworks. If you are working with concepts, then it is easier to find the mediums and materials that you will work with."

YIWOOO | Hong Kong, China

· **YIWOOO** ·

YIWOOO is a bamboo craft brand. The establishment of YIWOOO aims to return bamboo weaving to purity and simplicity, and to bring the missing sense of touch to this era. There were many bamboo weaving factories in Hong Kong. However, after Hong Kong transitioned into a financial center, the price of land increased. Many traditional, expensive techniques cannot be used because of lower incomes. On the other hand, the earth is facing a severe environmental crisis. YIWOOO believes that environmental problems can be relieved by using natural products, rather than by using glue and plastic products. YIWOOO wants to share the beauty of bamboo with the world.

1. Please share with us your weaving process from conception to creation. What's the most important step of the process?

The most important step of bamboo weaving is learning from your predecessors. Many techniques were invented by our predecessors. While learning the techniques, we also need to apply our thoughts. Before weaving, I draw a lot of sketches, but most of them are useless because many questions come up during the process. When questions are raised, I consult my predecessors and then try again by using some techniques I have learned.

2. Please tell us a bit about your chosen techniques and how you use them.

I only studied for a little more than a year and I'm mainly self-taught. I want to share one technique called "挑壓" in Chinese. It is a commonly used technique. Through "挑壓" I can press the bamboo tightly and form a repeating pattern. The concept is a bit similar to knitting, repeating one step and finally forming the pattern.

3. As time passes, some traditional techniques of bamboo weaving must be hard to find. How did you learn bamboo weaving? Are you a self-taught weaver?

I bought some books from Japan and I also talked to some elder craftsmen about their weaving techniques. If you want to do one thing, you will naturally find ways to learn, just like a hungry child wants to find something to eat. Of course, what I have learned is not enough. I am still exploring.

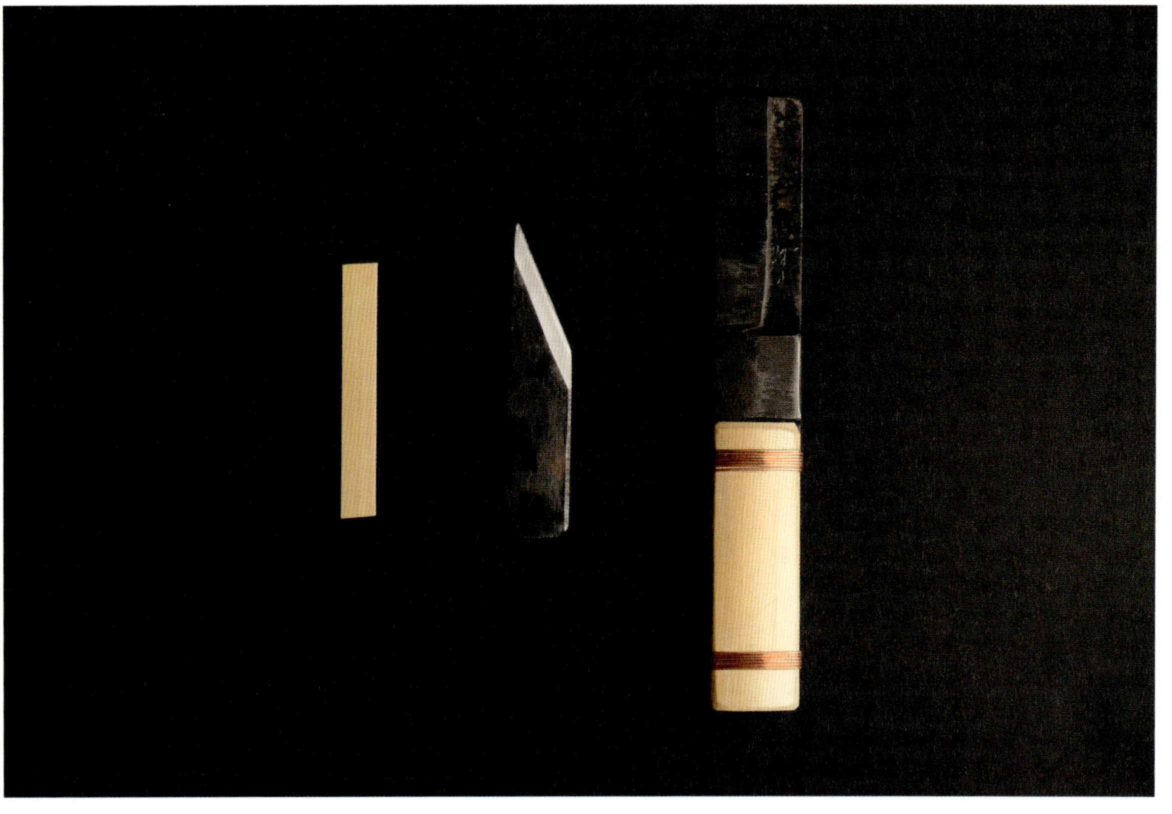

4. Could you please share with us the story of the most memorable product you have ever made?

There is a shoulder bag that looks simple, but it's very difficult to make. I failed many times in three months before I finished it. During the process, I kept testing the plasticity of bamboo. Different thicknesses of bamboo will affect the curvature and the choice of the manufacturing method. Even though the process of weaving the shoulder bag was difficult, I came to fully understand some techniques during the process.

5. All of your products are hand-woven. Is it time-consuming? What do you think of the value of hand-woven products?

Handicrafts have always been time-consuming. Japanese craftsmen can take weeks or months to complete a piece of work. The price of a piece of work does not only depend on the creator, but also the buyer. Therefore, we must communicate and share, to give everyone an understanding of the weaving process and the benefits of the work.

6. YIWOOO also teaches classes on bamboo weaving. What do you want to achieve through teaching?

Sharing and learning is the most direct way to convey bamboo culture and knowledge. Every city has its unique rhythm and atmosphere of life. In Hong Kong, for example, everything must be done in a short time under the rush of life. But finishing a bamboo knitting takes a long time. When you learn bamboo weaving, you are quietly adjusting your life rhythm. To learn one thing, we need to change the inherent rhythm. I also want to let everyone change his or her inherent rhythm through bamboo weaving.

‹ Insulation Pads with Hexagonal Chrysanthemum Weave

This is a traditional weaving technique. Based on the hexagonal weave, the 1.5m bamboo is woven into a chrysanthemum pattern, which is beautiful and practical.

Materials: bamboo, rattan

˄ Fruit Basket with Hexagonal Weave

This fruit basket with a hexagonal weave is soft and elastic. Bamboo is a natural material, suitable for dishware.

Materials: bamboo, rattan

Bamboo Shoulder Bag

This handmade bamboo shoulder bag is simple and minimalist. It is ultra-lightweight, key and ideal for carrying your day-to-night essentials. It fits your mobile phone, wallet, credit cards, keys, lip balm, etc.

Materials: bamboo, rattan, pure cotton canvas bag

Paper lamp.

INDEX

Aggeliki Dimitriadou

www.aggelikidimitriadou.com

P058–P065

Allyson Rousseau

www.allysonrousseau.com

P090–P097

Caroline Kaszak

woodhappen.com

P166–P173

Christina Christensen

www.christina-christensen.dk

P174–P181

Catriona Pollard

theartofweaving.com
P182–P189

Evee Erb

eveeerb.com
P122–P131

Hermine Van Dijck

herminevandijck.bigcartel.com
P016–P025

Hannah Waldron

www.hannahwaldron.co.uk
P132–P141

Julia Astreou

www.juliastreou.com
P042–P049

Kate Park

www.thekatepark.com
P142–P149

Morgan Hale

www.morgan-hale.com
P066–P073

María Hernández

www.instagram.com/mariamalatrama
P106–P113

Myriam Balaÿ

myriambalay.fr
P158–P165

Natalie Miller

www.nataliemillerdesign.com
P114–P121

Rie Endo

www.rocca-endo.com
P034–P041

Rina Matsumura

www.instagram.com/avelanewallart
P082–P089

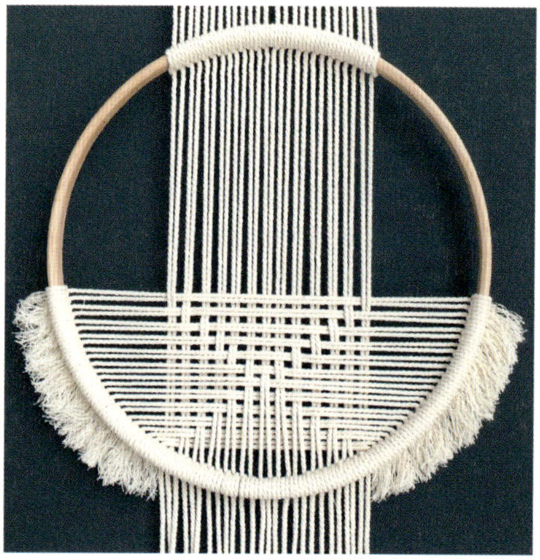

Studio Nom

studionom.nl/
P026–P033

Sarah Neubert

www.sarahneubert.com
P050–P057

Sally Blake

sallyblake.com
P198–207

Tammy Kanat

www.tammykanat.com
P074–P081

The Ninevites

theninevites.net
P098–P105

Tintsaba

www.tintsaba.com
P150–P157

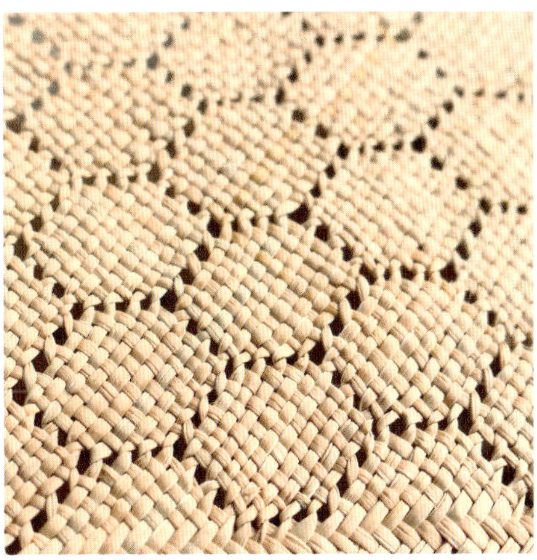

Taiwan Yuan-Li Handiwork Association

www.taiwanlin.org.tw
P190–P197

YIWOO

www.yiwooo.co
P208–P216

ACKNOWLE-DGEMENTS

We would like to express our gratitude to all of the artists for their generous contribution of images, ideas and concepts. We are also very grateful to many other people whose names do not appear in the credits, but who made specific contributions and provided support. Without them, the successful compilation of this book would not have been possible. Special thanks to all of the contributors for sharing their innovations and creativity with all of our readers around the world.